PRINTMAKING IN PARIS:
PICASSO AND HIS CONTEMPORARIES

Stephen Coppel

with contributions by Martin Hopkinson and Jane Lee

British Museum 1997

© Copyright The British Museum 1997
Designed by the British Museum Design Office

ISBN 0-86159 992-6

Front cover:
Pablo Picasso
Portrait de Jacqueline accoudée, au collier
Portrait of Jacqueline with necklace, resting on her elbow
1959 (catalogue number 157)
© Succession Picasso/DACS 1997

Back cover:
Raoul Ubac
Untitled
1953 (catalogue number 103)
© ADAGP, Paris and DACS, London 1997

PRINTMAKING IN PARIS:
PICASSO AND HIS CONTEMPORARIES

Catalogue of an exhibition at the British Museum
23 May - 14 September 1997

The exhibition will also be shown in reduced form at the
Hunterian Art Gallery, University of Glasgow, in 1998.

All prints in this exhibition are from the collection of the
Department of Prints and Drawings of the British Museum, with the
exception of 16 on loan from the Hunterian Art Gallery,
University of Glasgow.

CONTENTS

ACKNOWLEDGEMENTS

In preparing this publication the following are to be thanked: Martin Hopkinson, Curator of the Hunterian Art Gallery, University of Glasgow, researched and provided contributions to sections 5, 8 and 9, and Jane Lee, lecturer at Glasgow School of Art, to sections 6 and 7. For the new information they have unearthed, especially on artists in the post-1945 period, I am particularly grateful. Martin Hopkinson has kindly supervised the loan of 16 works from the collection of the Hunterian Art Gallery for this exhibition.

The following have generously offered information on artists included in this exhibition: Christian Germak, son-in-law of Edouard Goerg, Désirée Hayter on S. W. Hayter and Atelier 17, Guy Krohg on Pascin, Madame Christine Manessier on Alfred Manessier and Nono Reinhold. Other help was given by Elizabeth Miller of the Victoria & Albert Museum, Sophie Lefevrie and Dana Rowan.

No collection can be put together without the assistance of print dealers. In Paris our gratitude is extended to Arsène Bonafous-Murat, André Candillier, Galerie La Hune Brenner, Rosemarie Napolitano and Hubert Prouté; in London to Dr Frederick Mulder, Ian Mackenzie, Gordon Samuel of the Mercury Gallery, and Margaret Thornton and Richard Gault of the Redfern Gallery; in New York to Paul McCarron.

Delphine Picquet, a volunteer in the Department of Prints and Drawings in 1996, put together bibliographies of the artists and helped to organise the photography. Photography was undertaken by Graham Javes and Bill Lewis of Photographic Services. Victoria de Korda and Annette Pinto of the Conservation Department prepared the mounts for the exhibition.
Andrea Carr, editor, and Ann Lumley, graphic designer, of the Design Office must be thanked for producing this publication. Finally I am grateful to Antony Griffiths, Keeper and Frances Carey, Deputy Keeper, for their support of this exhibition and for the opportunity of developing the modern French print collection.

INTRODUCTION

An extraordinary ferment in printmaking took place among the avant-garde in Paris in the first half of this century. These years coincided with the prodigious creativity of Picasso, whose technical inventiveness and originality has made him the 20th-century's greatest artist-printmaker. As the world's undisputed art centre, Paris attracted an enormous influx of international artists. The numerous print workshops, together with an established system of dealer-publishers, encouraged artists to take up printmaking and contributed to the vitality and commercial success of the School of Paris.

Organised in ten sections (with each section in this catalogue prefaced by a brief introduction), this exhibition traces the principal episodes in the history of avant-garde printmaking in Paris between 1905 and the death of Picasso in 1973. It covers a period when the boundaries of art were being pushed by the Paris avant-garde in radically new directions. Although School of Paris painting is well documented, less attention has been directed to the prints produced by these artists. While the printmaking of particular artists and of certain movements like Cubism and Surrealism have received specialist study, no single overview of School of Paris printmaking has yet been made. This exhibition does not claim to present such an ambitious undertaking. Instead it attempts to map some of the contours of the history of the avant-garde print in Paris. However, it should be emphasised here that this is an exhibition of single-sheet prints and therefore printmaking for the illlustrated book, the *livre d'artiste*, which was an integral part of the printmaking of this period, is not represented.

The exhibition opens with the earliest prints of Picasso and Matisse at the time they first met at Gertrude Stein's apartment in Paris in 1906. At 37 Matisse was the elder artist; the Spanish-born Picasso, who had settled there in 1904, was 25. These two artists were to dominate the Paris avant-garde, although Matisse, unlike Picasso, remained an intermittent printmaker. The years from 1905 until the outbreak of the First World War were marked by the rise of the Fauve woodcut led by Matisse, Derain and Vlaminck and a wider interest in the woodcut shown by other avant-garde artists. The Cubist breakthrough of Picasso and Braque was paralleled in their etchings and drypoints from 1911-12. Their use of multiple viewpoints was adopted by a host of artists, such as Marcoussis, Laboureur, Villon and Dufresne, in their printmaking well into the 1920s.

The period between the wars saw a return to classical order and figuration exemplified in Picasso's *Vollard Suite*, Matisse's odalisque lithographs and the classical nudes of Derain and Galanis. It was also the period when Surrealist ideas were spread through the engravings produced by the many international artists who flocked to Atelier 17, Stanley Hayter's inspirational and collaborative workshop in Paris. The rise of Fascism and the outbreak of the Spanish Civil War became a major concern of Spanish expatriates like Picasso, Gonzalez and Miró and their sympathisers in Paris. By the time of the German Occupation in June 1940, many of the Paris avant-garde had already fled to America where they were to affect profoundly the development of the New York School.

After 1945 Paris resumed its position as the world's art capital, although by the early 1960s New York had taken over this title. With the availability of print workshops employing highly skilled printers like those of Mourlot for lithography and Lacourière for etching, Paris post-war saw the growth and dissemination of School of Paris printmaking through the commercial enterprise of print publishers. A reaction to the 'good taste' of such print publishing ventures as *Guilde de la Gravure* and *L'Oeuvre Gravé* were the prints of the Cobra artists and their followers in the 1950s. By this period Paris avant-garde printmaking was dominated by gestural abstraction, mostly expressed in colour lithographs and screenprints.

Picasso's printmaking after 1945 continued to be inventive and experimental until his death, exhausting the possibilities of each technique he took up. In 1945 he collaborated with the printers at Mourlot's workshop to produce lithographs in which he radically transformed the image as the stone was reworked from one state to the next. In the late 1950s he worked obsessively with the printer Arnéra making linocuts which were printed in several colours as he progressively cut away at the block. Picasso's extraordinary energy culminated in the hundreds of etchings he produced in the 1960s with Atelier Crommelynck. They had set up their workshop next door to his home at Mougins in order to minister to his insatiable appetite for printmaking.

The foundation of the British Museum's modern French print collection was laid by the bequest of Campbell Dodgson, a former Keeper of the Department of Prints and Drawings, in 1949. In recent years the Department has been strengthening its collection of Picasso prints made after 1945. The focus has been to seek key examples which reveal his originality as a printmaker, his preoccupation with themes reworked in different techniques and the collaborative relationship he enjoyed with printers during his long career.

Henri Matisse
Visage légèrement penché vers la gauche
Face slightly tilted to the left
1913 (catalogue number 8)
© Succession H Matisse/DACS 1997

Picasso had made only one etching in Barcelona before he settled in Paris in 1904, establishing himself at the Bateau Lavoir studio in the rue Ravignan, Montmartre. Although he had received no formal training in printmaking, his first etching in Paris was the masterpiece **Le Repas frugal** (catalogue number 1), which has become an icon of his Blue period. It was printed by Delâtre, the first of a series of printers with whom Picasso sustained a close and creative collaboration. His prints from these early years in Paris were all etchings or drypoints and parallel the themes of his paintings from the so-called Blue and Pink periods.

Although Matisse had tried out a few drypoints around 1900, his first serious venture in printmaking was in 1906 when he made his extraordinary series of lithographs (catalogue numbers 5-7). These coincided with his studies for his ground-breaking painting, **Joie de vivre**. A few woodcuts were made in this year as well, but Matisse preferred lithography as it gave greater facility for exploring his interest in line. A second series followed in 1913. Affected by the outbreak of the First World War and unable to work on large-scale canvasses, Matisse turned to making small etched portraits of his friends and family (catalogue numbers 9-10).

Pablo Picasso
1881-1973

1   *Le Repas frugal*
The frugal repast, 1904
Etching. 2nd state. 463 x 377mm.
Bloch 1; Baer 2.IIb.2.
1949-4-11-4624
Bequeathed by Campbell Dodgson

This image of an emaciated couple in a cheap wine shop is a technical *tour de force*. It was made in September 1904, at the start of Picasso's extraordinary career as a printmaker. This etching was made on a recycled plate which Picasso had scraped down. (Vestiges of an earlier landscape etching by Joan Gonzalez, a fellow Spaniard at the Bateau Lavoir, are still visible in the upper right.) Turning the plate round from a landscape to a portrait format, Picasso produced this astonishing image of human misery and loneliness. It is related to the paintings of his Blue period begun the previous year in Barcelona, in particular to **The blind man's meal**, 1903, (Metropolitan Museum of Art, New York).

About 30 proofs were pulled by the professional printer Delâtre in the autumn of 1904 and offered for sale by the Paris dealer Clovis Sagot at rue Lafitte. In 1913, the picture dealer and publisher Ambroise Vollard, who also had premises on rue Lafitte, bought fifteen of Picasso's early plates, including this one and catalogue numbers 2-4. These were steel-faced and printed by Louis Fort in a large edition of 250 for Vollard in 1913. The Vollard edition was widely distributed and ensured Picasso's reputation as a printmaker from an early date. This impression is from the 1913 edition.

2   *Tête de femme: Madeleine*
Head of a woman: Madeleine, 1905
Etching. Verso: inscribed in pencil: *Campbell Dodgson*. 121 x 90mm.
Bloch 2; Baer 3b.2.
1949-4-11-4625
Bequeathed by Campbell Dodgson

Made in January 1905, this small etching was Picasso's second print made in Paris. Unlike **Le Repas frugal**, it was etched on copper, a material which was more expensive than zinc; this probably accounts for its small size. Delâtre printed about a dozen proofs. This impression however is after steel-facing and comes from the 1913 Vollard edition. The subject is believed to be Madeleine, a model who appears in several of Picasso's works from the summer of 1904 and with whom Picasso was having an affair. Her hairstyle and her slender form recall the Tate Gallery's **Girl in a chemise**, an oil painting of 1904.

3 *Buste d'homme*
Bust of a man, 1905
Drypoint before steel-facing. Signed and
dated *2-05* on the plate. Signed in pencil.
120 x 93mm. Bloch 4; Baer 5a.
1949-4-11-4627
Bequeathed by Campbell Dodgson

This drypoint, made in February 1905, is
the first example of Picasso dating his work
directly on the plate, a practice which later
became commonplace in his printmaking.
Unlike catalogue numbers 1 and 2, this
impression is one of about a dozen proofs
printed by Delâtre before the plate was
steel-faced. Steel-facing was used to help
preserve the velvety burr of the drypoint
line which easily became worn through the
process of printing. Here the burr thrown
up by the drypoint tool has printed a rich
smudgy line, particularly noticeable on the
lower neck and shoulder.

A rough outline sketch of a woman, turned
three-quarters to the left, with her hair in a
chignon, is visible beneath the narrow
profile. The skinny shoulders and hairstyle
suggest that this was another depiction of
Madeleine. Picasso then changed his mind
and produced this androgynous male bust.
This print records the transition that was
taking place in his painting when the
saltimbanque, or acrobat, emerged as a
major theme.

4 *Salomé*
Salome, 1905
Drypoint. Signed and dated on the plate.
400 x 348mm. Bloch 14; Baer 17.IIIb.2.
1949-4-11-4630
Bequeathed by Campbell Dodgson

Made sometime in the latter half of 1905,
this drypoint was later steel-faced for the
1913 Vollard edition. The difference in the
quality of richness of line is apparent
between this print and *Buste d'homme*
(catalogue number 3). The monstrous
figure of Herod seated at left was
appropriated from an earlier drypoint of a
fat saltimbanque resting on a circus box.
Herod is shown watching the lithe dance of
the naked Salome while a kneeling
attendant offers on a platter the
decapitated head of John the Baptist.

Henri Matisse
1869-1954

5   *Nu mi-allongé, bras repliés vers les yeux*
Half-length nude, arms bent towards eyes, 1906
Lithograph on smooth japan paper.
Signed with initials on the stone.
Numbered *24/25* in ink. 432 x 245mm.
Duthuit 392.
1949-4-11-3348
Bequeathed by Campbell Dodgson

6   *Nu accroupi, profil à la chevelure noire*
Crouching nude in profile with black hair, 1906
Lithograph on smooth japan paper.
Signed with initials on the stone.
Numbered *1/25* in pencil. 422 x 215mm.
Duthuit 395.
1984-7-14-16

Shown here are three lithographs (catalogue numbers 5-7) from a series of fifteen which Matisse made in 1906. They show his Italian model Rosa Arpino in different, often unconventional, poses. In a few expressive and fluent lines, Matisse notes the essential volume and form of her body. They are the first lithographs he made and were produced while working on preparatory studies for his ambitious painting *Joie de vivre* (Barnes Foundation, Merion, Pennsylvania). Instead of working directly on the stone, Matisse used transfer paper which enabled him to draw freely from the model without having to consider her pose being reversed when printed. They were transferred to the stone and printed by Auguste Clot in editions of 25. The choice of a yellowish japan paper allowed even the wispiest line of the lithographic crayon to remain visible on the sheet. In 1908, these lithographs were included in Matisse's first American exhibition at Alfred Stieglitz's 291 gallery in New York, where a shocked public was disturbed by their boldness. *The New York Sun* exclaimed:

'With three furious scratches he can give you the female animal in all her shame and horror.' (cited in Alfred H. Barr, *Matisse: His Art and His Public* (1951), London, 1975, p. 114)

7   *Nu au pied droit sur un tabouret*
Nude with right foot on stool,
1906
Lithograph on smooth japan paper.
Signed with initials on the stone. Signed
and numbered *5/25* in ink. 415 x 193mm.
Duthuit 404.
1984-7-14-17

Matisse's comments on life drawing are
recorded in notes made by his pupil Sarah
Stein in 1908:

'Remember that a foot is a bridge. Consider
these feet in the ensemble. ...This straight
leg goes through the torso and meets the
shoulder as it were at a right angle. The
other leg, on which the model is also
standing, curves out and down like a flying
buttress of a cathedral...' ('Sarah Stein's
Notes, 1908' in Jack Flam, *Matisse on Art*,
rev. ed., Berkeley and Los Angeles:
University of California Press, 1995, p. 46)

This series of lithographs seems to move
through the poses of the model not unlike
the rhythmic movements of a dance.
Matisse was acutely aware of the analogy
of his drawings to music and dance,
remarking to his students in 1908:

'The lines must play in harmony and
return, as in music. You may flourish about
and embroider, but you must return to your
theme in order to establish the unity
essential to a work of art.' (Flam 1995, p. 49)

8   *Visage légèrement penché vers la gauche*
Face slightly tilted to the left,
1913
Lithograph on smooth japan paper.
Signed with initials on the stone. Signed
and numbered *30/50* in ink. 490 x 324mm.
Duthuit 414.
1949-4-11-3351
Bequeathed by Campbell Dodgson

Matisse did not return to lithography until
1913 when he made eight transfer
lithographs of the female nude. The model
for this print was Germaine Raynal, the
wife of the Cubist critic Maurice Raynal, a
close friend of Juan Gris. Like the 1906
series, this group was printed by Clot on a
similar japan paper but in an edition twice
the size. Larger in scale than the earlier
series, the 1913 lithographs are
extraordinary for the assured placing of
the figure on the sheet. Matisse's flowing
and seemingly effortless line was
fundamental to his art:

'One must always search for the desire of
the line, where it wishes to enter or where
to die away. Also always be sure of its
source; this must be done from the model.'
('Sarah Stein's Notes, 1908' in Flam 1995, p.
48)

In this print Matisse takes account of the
vertical format and size of the paper: by
cropping the top of the model's head and
allowing her breasts to rest on the bottom
edge of the sheet, Matisse heightens the
expressive impact of the composition.

9   *Josette Gris "Jeune Marin"*
Josette Gris "Young Sailor",
1914/15
Etching on greyish chine collé mounted
on white wove paper. Signed and
numbered *14/15* in ink. 160 x 61mm.
Duthuit 60.
1949-4-11-2571
Bequeathed by Campbell Dodgson

Whereas lithography was used for his
studies of the female nude, Matisse turned
to etching for his small informal portraits
of his friends and family. Although he had
made a few earlier attempts, it was not
until 1914 that etching was taken up with
serious interest. Over the next two years he
produced more than 60 etchings and
drypoints. These are mostly rapid, intimate
sketches, like this one of Josette Gris, the
wife of Juan Gris, whom he had met in the
summer of 1914. In all he made seven
etchings of Josette Gris; her jaunty sailor
collar prompted the title of this print. The
printing of Matisse's portrait etchings was
entrusted to Wittmann-Braun, printers at
rue Tournefort, Paris, who produced small
editions of 15. As with this print, these
editions were printed on grey chine collé, a
very fine china tissue glued to the paper
support. This provided a flat background
tone that revealed even the most lightly
etched line.

10   *Margot en kimono*
Margot in kimono, 1915
Etching on light grey chine collé
mounted on wove paper. Signed with
initials on the plate. Signed and
numbered *6/10* in pencil.
195 x 108mm. Duthuit 68.
On loan from the Hunterian Art Gallery,
University of Glasgow. J.A. McCallum
Collection, Acc. no. 3267

Matisse often used his daughter
Marguerite (also known as Margot) as a
model. Here she is posed in a splendid
Japanese kimono embroidered with carp
whose swirling movements follow her
wrapped form. Matisse delighted in
dressing his models in exotic costume. In
his etchings of this period, he adopted the
narrow upright format of Japanese prints,
which he greatly admired.

Albert Marquet
L'Homme heureux
The happy man
About 1903 (catalogue number 12)

THE WOODCUT FROM FAUVISM TO THE FIRST WORLD WAR

The term Fauve, meaning 'wild beast', was first used by the critic Louis Vauxcelles to describe his reaction to the violently coloured paintings of Matisse, Derain, Marquet, Vlaminck, Dufy and others at the 1905 Salon d'Automne in Paris. While the high-key colours of Fauvism were a feature of their painting, printmaking among these artists was largely confined to the black-and-white woodcut. Using the basic materials of wood, penknife and gouge, the Fauves' interest in this simple and direct technique coincided with their discovery of African tribal sculpture and Oceanic masks and carvings.

The Fauve woodcuts do not express the highly charged emotional states nor the nihilism and anxiety found in the contemporary woodcuts of the German Expressionists. Instead the Fauves were inspired by the primitivising woodcuts of Gauguin, particularly the Noa Noa prints, shown in the major retrospective at the Salon d'Automne in 1906, which included his wood carvings and reliefs. The Gauguin retrospective revealed to the Fauves the expressive potential of the woodblock and the power of primitive imagery. The woodcut continued to fascinate the avant-garde up to the First World War. Inspired by the French tradition of popular art, Dufy's highly decorative woodcuts were also widely disseminated as printed fabric designs, paving the way for the rise of post-war Art Deco.

Henri Matisse
1869-1954

11 *Le Grand Bois*
Large woodcut, 1906
Woodcut on laid paper. Signed with
initials on the block. Signed and
numbered *31/50* in ink. 475 x 380mm.
Duthuit 317.
1949-4-11-3763
Bequeathed by Campbell Dodgson

Full of Fauve energy and vitality, this
woodcut shows a nude reclining on a
deckchair covered with a polka-dotted
fabric. It is the largest and most important
of the four woodcuts that Matisse made in
his career, all of them cut with the help of
his wife between 1906 and 1907. Printed by
Auguste Clot, who also printed his
lithographs during this period (see
catalogue numbers 5-7), they are akin to
the ink brush drawings Matisse was
making at this time.

The original woodblock for this print is in
the Victoria & Albert Museum. From a
study of the block, it is clear that gouges of
different width were used to remove the
unwanted areas. The large expanse of the
nude's body was carved quite deeply with a
broad tool. In contrast the swirling lines of
the background were cut as a maze of
shallow channels. The only decorative
details are the model's earring and the
crude polka-dot pattern on the deckchair.
The artist's initials are disguised, lower
left, as part of the overall design. Whereas
Matisse's lithographs of this period are
spare and linear, the woodcuts come closest
in spirit to his Fauve paintings.

Albert Marquet
1875-1947

Born in Bordeaux, Marquet trained under
Moreau at the Ecole des Beaux-Arts in
Paris, where he met his fellow pupil
Matisse with whom he formed a close
artistic friendship. He painted his most
intensely Fauve pictures between 1905-06;
many of these were views of Le Havre and
other Normandy sea ports. Unlike Matisse,
he was a sporadic printmaker but among
his earliest prints are catalogue numbers
12 and 13, from around 1903. The style of
his calligraphic sketches prompted Matisse
to once remark: 'When I see Hokusai, I
think of Marquet, and vice versa.'

12 *L'Homme heureux*
The happy man, about 1903
Woodcut on thin cream wove paper.
Signed in ink. 128 x 91mm.
1994-12-11-6

This and catalogue number 13 are very rare
trial proofs for a projected illustrated
edition of Charles-Louis Philippe's *Bubu de
Montparnasse*, a sharply observed novel of
Paris prostitution, first published in 1901.
Around 1903, Philippe asked Marquet to
provide illustrations for a new edition.
From the café terraces Marquet made rapid
ink sketches of the passing Montparnasse
street life. This woodcut shows the pimp
Bubu striding down the street and offers a
visual parallel to the following passage
from the novel:

'I am Maurice, also known as Bubu of
Montparnasse. Maurice is a man who takes
women in his hand and moulds them.'
(Charles-Louis Philippe, *Bubu de
Montparnasse* (1901), translated by Cedric
Harrald, London 1960, p. 38)

Although the projected edition was never
realised in Marquet's lifetime, his widow
finally brought out a text illustrated with
reproductions of his sketches in 1958.

13 *La Veuve*
The widow, about 1903
Woodcut on thin cream wove paper.
Signed in ink. 176 x 105mm.
1994-12-11-7

This woodcut of a young woman in widow's weeds refers to a passage in *Bubu de Montparnasse* where the prostitute Berthe, already fatally ill with syphilis, needs to earn her mourning dress for her father's funeral by plying her trade on the streets.

'She walked for three hours, her feet on the stones ... She remembered it all: the boulevard walk, the alcohol of the cafés, the tasteless kisses ... and in her memory all these nights were the night of her father's interment.' (*Ibid*, pp. 74-5)

Crudely printed with inky margins, these two impressions formerly belonged to Gustav Schiefler, a Hamburg judge and important collector of German Expressionist prints, who first catalogued the work of Munch and Kirchner. Undoubtedly struck by their expressionist quality, he was given the two prints by Marquet on a visit to Paris in 1911.

Louis Valtat
1869-1952
Born into a wealthy Dieppe family, Valtat trained under Moreau at the Ecole des Beaux-Arts and then at the Académie Julian. From the late 1890s Valtat's painting seemed to foreshadow Fauvism but his use of pure colour never displayed the exuberance and violent brushwork of Matisse, Derain and Vlaminck. The *Femmes* suite can be dated around 1903-05 when Valtat painted a number of nudes and bathers in high-key colour. Always open to other influences, Valtat remained on the fringes of Fauvism.

14 **A group of nudes**, from *Femmes*, 1903-05
Woodcut printed in red with touches of green watercolour, on simili-japan paper. Signed with initials in pencil.
166 x 185mm.
On loan from the Hunterian Art Gallery, University of Glasgow. Acc. no. 48047

15 **A group of nudes**, from *Femmes*, 1903-05
Woodcut printed in red with touches of yellow watercolour, on simili-japan paper. Signed with initials in pencil.
168 x 185mm.
On loan from the Hunterian Art Gallery, University of Glasgow. Acc. no. 48049

These come from an exceptionally rare suite of eight woodcuts known as *Femmes*. Whereas most Fauve woodcuts were printed in black-and-white, Valtat's suite is unusual in its use of colour. Individual woodcuts from the Hunterian set are crudely printed in red, blue, mauve, crimson and pale green. All are lightly touched with wash, often in complementary colours. In catalogue number 14, the festoon stretched above the nudes is hand-coloured in green. In catalogue number 15, yellow watercolour is used to pick out the upper left nude's flow of blonde hair. It is not known how many suites were made but the number must have been very small. Never published as an album, the Hunterian set is numbered *2* on the front wrapper. Another set, numbered *1*, is in the Bibliothèque Nationale, Paris.

Maurice de Vlaminck
1876-1958

16 *Au Bordel*
    At the brothel, about 1906
    Woodcut touched with brush and wash,
    on cream wove paper. Signed with the
    brush in ink . 245 x 179mm.
    Walterskirchen 1.
    1982-6-19-22

The block for this print came from a piece
of wood ripped from the toilet of
Vlaminck's studio, which he shared with
Derain at Chatou, a suburb of Paris. Made
purely for his own diversion, only a few
proofs were printed by Vlaminck at the
time. The primitivism of this print and
catalogue number 17 reveals the impact of
Vlaminck's discovery of African and
Oceanic art about 1905, when he became an
early champion and collector of tribal
sculpture. His collection of masks and
fetishes excited much interest from Derain
and Matisse. This impression was printed
before the 1920 edition of 100 published by
Florent Fels for a deluxe issue of the Paris
art journal *Action* (no. 4, July 1920). More
of the thighs of the central figure and of
the legs of the left figure are shown on this
impression suggesting that the block was
shortened at the base for the Fels edition.
Vlaminck used brush and black wash to
extend and reinforce the printed borderline
on this impression.

17 *Tête de femme*
    Head of a woman, about 1906
    Woodcut on simili-japan paper. Signed in
    black crayon. 99 x 158mm.
    Walterskirchen 2
    On loan from the Hunterian Art Gallery,
    University of Glasgow. Acc. no. 21217

The mask-like face and the expressive
distortion of this woodcut reveal
Vlaminck's indebtedness to African tribal
wood sculpture. In 1904-05, Vlaminck
painted several portraits of prostitutes as
well as writing two novels of prostitute life
in Paris, *D'un lit dans l'autre* (1902, written
in collaboration with Fernand Sernada)
and *Tout pour ça* (1903), both of which were
illustrated by Derain. These two woodcuts
are related to this interest. Like **Au
Bordel**, the block for this print was cut
around 1906. In 1958, it was printed by
Erkerpresse in St Gallen in an edition of 50
for the Swiss publisher Bodensee-Verlag.
This impression, which is unnumbered and
without the publisher's drystamp, is
outside the 1958 edition.

André Derain
1880-1954

18   *Frise*
Frieze, 1906
Woodcut on laid paper. Signed in pencil.
70 x 245mm. Adhémar 13.
1997-4-27-1

Like Vlaminck, with whom he shared the studio at Chatou, Derain was fascinated by tribal art. In March 1906, while on a visit to London, Derain wrote to Vlaminck of his excitement at seeing the British Museum's ethnographic collections, which he called the 'Musée nègre':

'It is phenomenal, bewitching in its expressiveness.' (André Derain, *Lettres à Vlaminck*, Paris, 1955, letter dated 7 March [1906], pp. 196-7)

This woodcut dates from 1906 when Derain took up the technique; an interest which culminated in his illustrations for Apollinaire's *L'Enchanteur pourrissant* published in 1909. Derain appears to have been directly inspired by Gauguin's Noa Noa woodcuts and his Marquesan wood reliefs and carvings on view at the 1906 retrospective at the Salon d'Automne. The print shown here is one of about twenty single-sheet woodcuts Derain made during this period; printed in a tiny number of proofs, they were never published by a dealer in an edition.

Othon Friesz
1879-1949

The son of a sea-captain, Friesz became friends with Dufy and Braque who were fellow students at the Ecole des Beaux-Arts in Le Havre and later in Paris. The highpoint of his Fauve work occurred in 1905 when he painted with Dufy in the Normandy ports and with Braque in Antwerp and L'Estaque the following year. Friesz made very few prints before 1914; these were all woodcuts based on his oil paintings.

19   *Le Pêcheur de Cassis*
The fisherman of Cassis, 1910
Woodcut on thin greyish wove paper. Signed and dated *Xbre 1910* in pencil.
205 x 152mm.
1985-11-9-8

Friesz may have begun this woodcut after the high praise given to his painting of this composition by Apollinaire when it was shown at the Salon d' Automne in October 1910. The poet singled out the picture as:

'... one of the artist's best works. ...There is a great deal of humanity in this old man, who has been worn out by storms and whose eyes reflect distant lands. And the background, with the sea, and a ship, serves to sustain the emotion.'
(*L'Intransigeant* (1 October 1910) in Guillaume Apollinaire, *Chroniques d'art 1902-1918*, Paris: Gallimard, 1960, pp. 153-4)

Unlike most Fauve prints, this impression is inscribed by the artist with a date; October 1910. Friesz later cut a monogram of his initials on the block, an example is in the Bibliothèque Nationale.

Raoul Dufy
1877-1953

20 *La Danse*
The Dance, 1910
Woodcut on thin greyish laid paper.
Titled on the block. Signed and numbered
87/100 in pencil. 313 x 317mm.
1993-6-20-15

This and *L'Amour* (catalogue number 21)
come from a set of four woodcuts made
early in 1910; the other two are *La Chasse*
and *La Pêche*. They were made shortly
after Dufy's return from Munich where he
had first encountered the woodcuts of
Kandinsky and the *Blaue Reiter* group
during the winter of 1909-10. Dufy's
woodcuts were shown at the Salon
d' Automne in October 1910 where
Apollinaire writing in *L'Intransigeant*
(1 October 1910) described them as
'beautiful and very decorative'. Also shown
were several proofs of Dufy's woodcut
illustrations to Apollinaire's *Le Bestiaire*,
which was published the following year.
Dufy exploited the decorative possibilities
of the woodcut by cutting white-line
hatchings out of the block with gouges and
pen knife. The block itself is composed of
several endgrain pieces bolted together, the
joins of which can still be seen. The figures
in these woodcuts are placed within a
setting of abundant vegetation. Here,
among tropical palm trees, a sailor and a
Calypso woman dance to the
accompaniment of a grinning accordion-
player; the ship waiting in the bay is a
reminder that their pleasure is transient.
During the 1920s this composition was used
on a fabric printed by the Lyons silk
manufacturers Bianchini-Férier.

21 *L'Amour*
Love, 1910
Woodcut on heavy japan paper. Titled on
the block. Signed and numbered *21/100* in
pencil. 306 x 314mm.
1993-6-20-16

Here an Arcadian idyll replaces the
exoticism of the French Caribbean. In a
garden teeming with growth and fecundity,
a couple make love; the stylised flowers and
leaves make playful reference to classical
vase decoration, while the lovers are
rhymed by the pair of buzzing insects
overhead. The prints shown here come
from the first edition of 1910 which was
lightly printed on chine volant or japan
paper. Two later editions, one from the
early 1950s and another from the 1960s,
were printed heavily in solid black with a
loss of detail in the more finely cut lines.

22 *Tirez les premiers, messieurs
les Français!*
**Shoot first, gentlemen of
France!**, 1915
Woodcut on thin wove paper. Signed with
monogram on the block; title printed
below image. 472 x 382mm.
On loan from the Hunterian Art Gallery,
University of Glasgow. Acc. no. 40901

A Scottish regiment commander invites his
French ally to fire the first shot at the
German helmets peeping over the trenches;
a startled hare bolts out of the line of fire.
This is one of several light-hearted
patriotic prints which Dufy made in 1915,
when following enlistment he served as a
driver for the army postal service. It was
first published in *Le Mot* (13 February
1915), the magazine founded by Jean
Cocteau on 28 November 1914, with the
avowed purpose of 'rescuing modernism
from too much affiliation with Germany'.
Dufy's patriotic prints were inspired by the
'images de Epinal', the French popular
woodcuts of the Napoleonic period. This
print was also available in a de luxe edition
of 100 printed on japan paper; these sold
separately at 5 francs each.

Marie Laurencin
1885-1956

Laurencin was introduced to Picasso through Braque in 1907. An intimate of the Bateau Lavoir group, she met the poet Apollinaire with whom she maintained a close liaison for six years, until December 1912. This period coincided with the most avant-garde phase of her career. She exhibited with Jacques Villon, Gleizes, Metzinger and other advocates of Cubism at the Section d'Or exhibition at the Galerie La Boëtie in October 1912. After 1920, in the wake of her success as a painter, her prints became more conventional and were largely devoted to the illustration of *livres d'artiste*; these number some 41 books and albums.

23   *Grande tête de femme*
      Large female head, 1910
      Woodcut on thin oriental laid paper.
      Signed in pencil. 280 x 178mm.
      Marchesseau 19.
      1994-5-15-7

One of only a dozen woodcuts made in Laurencin's career, this print shows the influence of Picasso, who was a close friend. The woman's head is reduced to a simple bold oval while the features of her face are abstracted to a profile nose and staring eye. It belongs to the period between 1908 and 1912 when her printmaking was at its most experimental. Printed on a thin japanese paper, this impression may date from a later printing, possibly of the 1920s.

Jean-Emile Laboureur
1877-1943

Born and educated in Nantes, Laboureur's family prosperity gave him a measure of financial independence. He was taught wood-engraving by Auguste Lepère in Paris but his knowledge of prints was widened by periods of study in the print rooms of Dresden and the British Museum. Between 1903 and 1908 he lived in the United States. It was only after settling in Paris in 1910 when he came in contact with the avant-garde, which included Apollinaire, Max Jacob, Dufy and Laurencin (who remained a close friend and confidante for many years), that a modern note is struck in his prints.

24   *Lassitude*, 1912
      Colour woodcut on laid paper. Signed on the block. Signed and inscribed: *épreuve d'essai* in pencil. 241 x 270mm.
      Laboureur 682.
      1994-6-19-20

In this extraordinary woodcut, Laboureur has created an image of drug addiction: the woman's languor is opium induced; the strange grey eye-sockets suspended like shades above her face convey her dreamy state. This was printed from a single block with water-based inks in an edition of 35 by Féquet in 1914. In this trial proof the woman's head is outlined in black, an orange accent separates the parted lips, and stripes of yellow across the forehead suggest a fringe of blonde hair. It was first shown with three other woodcuts by Laboureur at the Salon des Indépendants in 1913. Apollinaire, in a review of the 1912 Salon d' Automne, singled out Laboureur's woodcuts as 'very modern in feeling'. Indeed, *Lassitude* uncannily anticipates the image of modern woman found in the novels of Aldous Huxley and other writers of the 1920s.

Félix Vallotton
1865-1925

Born in Switzerland, Vallotton established his reputation as one of the leading graphic artists in Paris during the 1890s, where his striking use of black-and-white patterns and bold silhouettes was emulated by other artists including Laboureur. *C'est la guerre!* is the only significant example of printmaking by Vallotton after 1901.

25 *C'est la guerre!*
    This is War!, 1915-16
    Album cover edged with black cloth and spattered with red ink. The six woodcuts in the album are printed on wove paper. Each print is signed with initials on the block and also signed and numbered *67/100* in pencil. Each image measures 177 x 224mm. Vallotton-Goerg 212-17
    1993-10-3-24.1-6

26 *La Tranchée*
    The trench, 1915
    Plate 1 from the album *C'est la guerre!*.
    Vallotton-Goerg 212.
    1993-10-3-24.1

27 *L'Orgie*
    The orgy, 1915
    Plate 2 from the album *C'est la guerre!*.
    Vallotton-Goerg 213.
    1993-10-3-24.2

28 *Les Fils de fer*
    Iron wires, 1916
    Plate 3 from the album *C'est la guerre!*.
    Vallotton-Goerg 214.
    1993-10-3-24.3

29 *Le Guetteur*
    The lookout, 1916
    Plate 5 from the album *C'est la guerre!*.
    Vallotton-Goerg 216.
    1993-10-3-24.5

This album of six woodcuts, four of which are shown here, was published and sold in an edition of 100 by Vallotton himself. Prompted by the success of Dufy's patriotic woodcuts (see catalogue number 22), Vallotton exploited the French popular print tradition to rouse patriotic sentiment during the First World War. This explains the cartoon-like character of Vallotton's album. His experience as a voluntary stretcher-bearer at the Front directly informs the album. The black-edged cover of *C'est la guerre!* is spattered with red ink in imitation of blood. The random violence of modern trench warfare is evoked in the opening plate with the sudden explosion on a desolate battlefield. Catalogue number 28 shows corpses of soldiers bloated and entangled in wire; snow falling from a night sky will eventually bury them. The other subjects in the album are German soldiers in a drunken orgy (catalogue number 27), a deadly encounter between two soldiers at night, the night lookout keeping watch in the driving rain (catalogue number 29), and a French family cowering in the wine cellar of their farmhouse. Despite their topical subject matter, the album at 85 francs failed to find many buyers, provoking Vallotton to record in his journal on 18 February 1916:

'It is true that this is war! ... and that pockets are not easily opened for something that is not a work of solidarity - And yet this is one'.

(cited by Deborah Goodman in *Félix Vallotton*, exhibition catalogue with an introduction and essay by Sasha Newman, New Haven, Yale University Art Gallery, 1992, p. 195)

Chana Orloff
1888-1968

Born in the Ukraine and brought up in Petah Tiqwa, Palestine's first Jewish colony, Orloff arrived in Paris in 1910. She mixed freely with many of the Montparnasse painters and poets including Picasso, Apollinaire, Cocteau and Modigliani before marrying the poet Ary Justman in 1916. She began making portrait busts in wood from 1913. From the early 1920s she made her reputation as a leading portrait sculptor of the Paris artistic and cultural élite. Her preferred medium was wood, although she also sculpted in stone, marble and bronze. In 1923 she published a second album of 41 portrait woodcuts of the leading figures of the Paris avant-garde entitled **Figures d'aujourd'hui**.

30   **Portrait de Mlle Watts**
Plate 3 from the portfolio of 11 woodcuts **Bois gravés de Chana Orloff**, 1919. Woodcut on thin machine wove paper. Lettered with title lower left. Signed in pencil. The portfolio is numbered *1/100* in ink on the colophon. 315 x 206mm. 1992-6-20-29.4

This is from Orloff's first portfolio of eleven woodcut portraits published by D'Alignan in Paris on 31 May 1919. The portfolio is the artist's personal tribute to the women who provided her with solidarity and support after the death of her husband Ary Justman earlier that year from Spanish influenza. Left to raise her one-year old son as a widowed mother, Orloff threw herself into her work. The woodcut shown here depicts Mlle Watts, a close friend. Orloff's interest in making woodcuts developed from her sculpture in wood. With a sculptor's understanding of materials, Orloff selected planks of wood with an interesting grain which could be exploited pictorially. Here, in **Mlle Watts**, the wood-grain is integral to expressing the sitter's fashionably wavy hairstyle while the jagged edges of the block give her tilted hat a coquettish look. The complete portfolio is in the British Museum; it was printed on the presses of Frazier-Soye on a cheap machine wove paper in an edition of 100.

In 1907 Picasso painted **Les Demoiselles d'Avignon** (Museum of Modern Art, New York), the most revolutionary picture of the 20th century. Apollinaire arranged for Braque to see the work in Picasso's studio at the Bateau Lavoir. The two artists became inseparable friends and collaborators in their experiments towards Cubism, with its radical departure from single-point perspective that had governed Western painting since the Renaissance. As Braque later recalled,

'We lived in Montmartre, we saw each other everyday, we talked... Picasso and I said things to each other during those years that no one says anymore.... We were like two mountain climbers roped together.' (cited in Burr Wallen and Donna Stein, *The Cubist Print*, Santa Barbara, University Art Museum, University of California, p. 23)

Their earliest Cubist prints were in etching and drypoint, which lent themselves to the graphic interpretation of interlocking planes and cubes. The analysis of form and volume, first signalled by Cézanne in his painting, was explored largely through the neutral motif of still life. While the most innovative years of Cubist etching were between 1909 and 1912, the style was taken up by many avant-garde artists in their printmaking. Among the most notable in etching were Villon, Marcoussis and Laurens. Even before the 1920s a diluted, more decorative version of Cubism was being spread through prints made by a host of artists, including Laboureur and Dufresne.

Josef Capek
Figure called Lelio
1913 (catalogue number 38)

André Derain
1880-1954

31 **Nu**
Nude, about 1909
Drypoint on laid paper. Inscribed in
pencil: *pour André Derain - Alice Derain*.
177 x 94mm. Adhémar 50.
1996-6-8-7

A nude bather stands between two trees;
the simplified landscape behind her is
composed of overlapping planes
reminiscent of Cézanne. Her features
derive from a Fang tribal mask which
Derain had bought from Vlaminck (see
catalogue number 16) in 1906 and later
showed to Picasso and Matisse. The mask
is now in the Musée National d' Art
Moderne, Pompidou Centre, Paris. When
Derain was away fighting at the Front, his
wife Alice would sign his work: *For André
Derain - Alice Derain*. This impression was
acquired by the Norwegian dealer Walter
Halvorsen, a former student of Matisse and
a supplier of Fauve pictures for
Scandinavian collectors, when he visited
Derain's studio in 1915.

Pablo Picasso
1881-1973

32 **Deux figures nues**
Two nude figures, 1909
Drypoint and scraper on laid paper. 3rd
state. Signed in pencil. 130 x 110mm.
Bloch 17; Baer 21.IIIb.
On loan from the Hunterian Art Gallery,
University of Glasgow. Acc. no. 21320

Picasso worked on this plate early in 1909.
Although it shows a boy offering a cup to a
seated woman with a guitar, Picasso's main
concern is not with the subject but in
reducing the figures to their essential
planar form, a development which is
paralleled in his painting. Printed after
steel-facing by Delâtre in an edition of 100,
this drypoint was published in 1912 by
Daniel-Henry Kahnweiler. The German-
born dealer and publisher, Kahnweiler
opened his first gallery at 28 rue Vignon
where he championed the Paris avant-
garde, most notably the work of Picasso,
Braque, Derain and Vlaminck.

33 **Nature morte au compotier**
Still life with fruit-dish, 1908-09
Drypoint and scraper on laid paper. 3rd
state. Signed and numbered *61* in pencil.
131 x 110mm. Bloch 22; Baer 22.IIIb.
1976-5-15-12

Also published by Kahnweiler in 1912, this
shows a still life composed of pears and
fruit-stand. Made in 1908-09, it marks the
early stages of Picasso's interest in still life
as a neutral vehicle for the analysis of form
and volume.

34 *Nature morte à la bouteille de Marc*
Still life with bottle of *Marc*, 1911
Drypoint on laid paper. Signed and numbered *38* in pencil. 500 x 305mm.
Bloch 24; Baer 33b.
1980-6-28-55

A highpoint of Picasso's analytical Cubist phase, the composition of this print is reduced to a series of interlocking and overlapping planes. From his Cubist painting Picasso introduces *passage*, a stylistic device which enables one plane to merge with another by leaving one side open. The placing of the lettering for the label *Marc*, a rough brandy, establishes the flatness of the picture plane. This and other motifs, such as the glasses and playing cards, make reference to the external world of the artists' café. This drypoint and a companion print by Braque entitled ***Fox*** are believed to have been worked on while both artists were staying in the Pyrenees in the late summer of 1911. Remarkable for its scale and invention, Picasso's drypoint was printed by Delâtre for Kahnweiler in an edition of 100 in 1912. Stamped with the collector's initials on the verso, this impression formerly belonged to Georges Bloch who compiled a catalogue raisonné of Picasso's prints, the first volume of which was published in 1968.

35 *L'Homme au chien (rue Schoelcher)*
Man with a dog, 1915
Etching and scraper on wove paper. Signed in red crayon. 278 x 218mm.
Bloch 28; Baer 39.IIIBb.
1982-7-24-15

Although the subject is a man reading a newspaper with a dog lying by his feet, Picasso's main purpose was in constructing the composition from a series of abstract planes. This development proceeded from his collages, or *papiers collés*, begun in the autumn of 1912 which heralded his synthetic Cubist phase. The rue Schoelcher mentioned in the etching's title refers to the place where Picasso was living with his consumptive mistress Eva Gouel who died in December 1915. Picasso worked on this plate in the spring of 1915 but it was not until after 1930 when Vollard acquired the plate that an edition of 100 was printed by Louis Fort.

Georges Braque
1882-1963

36 **_Job_**, 1911
Drypoint on Arches laid paper. Signed in
pencil. 143 x 199mm. Vallier 5.
On loan from the Hunterian Art Gallery,
University of Glasgow. Acc. no. 21164

Taking its title from the lettering on the
print, this was one of only two prints by
Braque to be published by Kahnweiler in
1912. The Cubist illusionism of Braque's
paintings is here translated into
printmaking, notably in the treatment of
shadow cast by the nail in the upper right
of this drypoint. An oblique reference to
the café world is invoked by the word _JOB_,
the brand name of a cigarette rolling paper.
This and Braque's **_Fox_** were not a
commercial success. The catalogue for the
1923 sale of Kahnweiler's stock, which had
been sequestrated as enemy property by the
French government during the First World
War, showed that out of an edition of 100
some 94 impressions of this print still
remained.

37 **_Nature morte I_**
Still life I, 1911 (printed in 1950)
Drypoint on Arches paper. Signed and
inscribed: _H.C._ in pencil. 345 x 219mm.
Vallier 8.
1975-10-25-4

Braque, in an interview of 1910, explained
how he arrived at still life:

'I couldn't portray a woman in all her
loveliness ... I haven't the skill. No one has.
I must, therefore, create a new sort of
beauty, the beauty that appears to me in
terms of volume, of line, of mass, of weight,
and through that beauty interpret my
subjective impression.' (cited in Jennifer
Mundy, _Georges Braque Printmaker_,
London, Tate Gallery, 1993, p. 13)

Unlike the prodigious output of Picasso,
printmaking for Braque was an
intermittent and painstaking activity.
Between 1907 and 1913 Braque made ten
prints, all of them etchings or drypoints.
Most of his prints were made after the
Second World War, when he was in his
sixties. While a few trial proofs of this
print were pulled in 1911, this impression
comes from the edition of 50 printed by
Visat for the publisher Maeght in 1950. The
abbreviation _H.C._ on this impression refers
to _Hors commerce_, meaning 'not for sale';
such proofs were printed extra to the
edition and were often reserved for the
publisher.

Josef Capek
1887-1945

A central figure in avant-garde Prague, Capek was a painter, printmaker, critic and editor, who was profoundly influenced by Picasso during regular visits to Paris between 1910 and 1911. By the end of the First World War Capek was turning his attention to social and political themes. He died in Belsen after five years in concentration camps.

38   *Figure called Lelio*, 1913
> Etching. Signed, dated and titled in pencil. 340 x 230mm.
> 1985-11-9-33
> Acquired by exchange from the National Gallery in Prague

Inspired by analytical Cubism, this etching shows the female figure reduced to a geometry of large planes placed at an oblique angle. It is after a painting by Capek now in the National Gallery, Prague. Achieved with short deft strokes, this etching bears a stylistic and compositional resemblance to Picasso's **Mlle Léonie**, which was one of the etched illustrations in *Saint Matorel*, a limited edition book published by Kahnweiler in 1911.

Gino Severini
1883-1966

39   *La Modiste*
      The dressmaker, 1916
> Linocut. Signed and numbered *2/15* in pencil. 190 x 130mm. Meloni 11.
> On loan from the Hunterian Art Gallery, University of Glasgow. Acc. no. 50212

Of the Italian Futurists, Severini had the closest affinity with Cubism and with the prismatic colour developments of Delaunay (see catalogue number 44). An early example of the linocut, a 20th-century technique, this print shows the influence of Picasso's synthetic Cubism in its collage-like build-up of planes. Severini based his forms on cut-outs, including dressmakers' patterns. It was first published in the Paris literary review *Sic* (nos 8-10, August-October 1916), although the letterpress above the print described it as 'the first woodcut of Gino Severini.' Also published in this review were the first woodcuts of Chana Orloff (catalogue number 30). This impression comes from the de luxe edition of 15 printed without lettering; it was available to collectors from the office of *Sic* and at Galerie Marseille, 16 rue de Seine.

Jean-Emile Laboureur
1877-1943

Petite images de la guerre sur le front britannique, 1917

The nine engravings in the album are printed on thin laid paper. Engraved title on each plate. Each print numbered *36* in pencil. Laboureur 144-152.IV.
1949-4-11-5069.1-9
Bequeathed by Campbell Dodgson

40   Plate 4: *Le Retour aux tranchées*
Return to the trenches, 1916
175 x 140mm. Laboureur 147.IV.
1949-4-11-5069.4

41   Plate 8: *Les Tranchées dans le village*
The trenches in the village, 1916
175 x 138mm. Laboureur 151.IV.
1949-4-11-5069.8

Fluent in English, Laboureur was assigned to the British Expeditionary Force as an interpreter from 1914 to 1916. He first took up burin engraving in 1915, using plates retrieved from British shell-cases. Shown here are two engravings from a suite of nine entitled **Petites images de la guerre sur le front britannique** produced the following year. While the hatched lines recall the old master engravings he had studied in London and Dresden (see catalogue number 24), Laboureur was successful in marrying an antique manner of engraving to a Cubist vocabulary. Published in an edition of 120, the engravings were printed in Paris by A. Vernant in August 1917. The album opens with an epigraph from Robert Burton's *The Anatomy of Melancholy* (first published in 1621):

'I hear new news every day, and those ordinary rumours of war, ... of towns taken, cities besieged in *France, Germany, Turkey, Persia, Poland, etc.*'

Campbell Dodgson, Keeper of Prints and Drawings at the British Museum, was a great admirer of Laboureur. The first major catalogue of Laboureur's engravings was dedicated by its compiler Godefroy to Dodgson, whose large personal collection was bequeathed to the Museum in 1949.

Louis Marcoussis
1878-1941

Born in Poland, Marcoussis changed his name from the Polish Markous at the suggestion of his friend Apollinaire. More proficient as an etcher than a painter, Marcoussis made his earliest Cubist etchings from 1911-12; these were brought to a wider public through the efforts of Apollinaire whose portrait he etched.

42   *Le Comptoir*
      Bar, 1920
      Etching, aquatint and drypoint. 4th state.
      Signed, dated and titled on the plate.
      187 x 142mm. Milet 35.IV.
      On loan from the Hunterian Art Gallery,
      University of Glasgow. Acc. no. 21177

In this etching Marcoussis uses the lettering *vins*, *hôtel* and *Paris* to allude to the bar and café world of Paris. Inspired by Picasso's synthetic Cubism, the composition is constructed from a series of overlapping planes which are differentiated by etching technique and tone. Made in 1920, this comes from the edition of 125 published two years later in the fourth portfolio of *Die Schaffenden*, the German review which mostly issued German Expressionist prints.

Albert Gleizes
1881-1953

An influential spokesman for Cubism, Gleizes wrote *Du Cubisme* with Jean Metzinger in 1912; it was the first book to explain the theoretical ideas behind the movement. A close friend of Delaunay and Villon, he was a key member of the Section d'Or which met in Villon's studio at Puteaux between 1911 and 1913. In the late 1920s, Gleizes fulfilled his ambition of establishing an artists' utopian community at Moly-Sabata on the Rhône.

43   ***Composition Cubiste***
      Cubist composition, 1921
      Lithograph. Signed and dated on the stone. Signed with initials in pencil. 362 x 267mm. Loyer 153
      On loan from the Hunterian Art Gallery, University of Glasgow. Acc. no. 21147

Like catalogue number 42, this was published in the fourth portfolio of *Die Schaffenden* and was the only lithograph made by Gleizes. With its overlapping planes and cut-out shapes, this is another example of synthetic Cubism inspired by Picasso.

Robert Delaunay
1885-1941

From 1912-13, Delaunay and his Russian-born wife Sonia Terk-Delaunay developed Orphism, an offshoot of Cubism, which was concerned with expressing motion and rhythm through coloured arcs and discs. To the Orphic group, which included the poet Blaise Cendrars, the Eiffel Tower served as the symbol of modernity and of metropolitan Paris.

44   *Vue aérienne de la Tour*
     Aerial view of the Eiffel Tower, 1926
     Lithograph on chine volant. Signed in pencil. 197 x 200mm. Loyer and Perussaux 8.
     On loan from the Hunterian Art Gallery, University of Glasgow. Acc. no. 21167

This is from a suite of twenty lithographs by Robert Delaunay which accompanied the deluxe edition of Joseph Delteil's *Allo! Paris!*, a *livre d'artiste* published by Editions des Quatre Chemins in 1926. Several of the lithographs in this book were based on paintings of the mid-1920s when Delaunay returned to the Eiffel Tower motif. In 1924, Cendrars wrote:

'There are so many points of view from which one can examine the phenomenon of the Eiffel Tower. But Delaunay wanted to interpret it plastically... He truncated it and he tilted it in order to disclose all of its three hundred dizzying meters of height. He adopted ten points of view, fifteen perspectives - one part is seen from above, another from below, ... from the height of a bird in flight, from the depths of earth itself... .' (cited in Burr Wallen and Donna Stein, *The Cubist Print*, Santa Barbara, University Art Museum, University of California, 1981, p. 58)

Charles Dufresne
1876-1938

45   *A la Guadeloupe*
     At Guadeloupe, about 1919
     Etching, drypoint with woodcut printed in yellow ochre. Signed on the plate. Signed, titled and numbered *11/25* in pencil, with publisher's blindstamp. 212 x 283mm. Dufresne 21.
     1927-2-12-139
     Presented by the Contemporary Art Society

Employing a Cubist vocabulary to a decorative end, Dufresne's most characteristic work was made in the 1920s. As in this print, his subjects are usually set in the tropics. Here the palm trees, the native women and flying fish invite the viewer to escape to a world of indolence and ease. Unusual in its combination of etching and woodcut, this print possesses a warmth and texture provided by the woodblock printed in yellow ochre. This impression was purchased for 50 francs by Campbell Dodgson on behalf of the Contemporary Art Society from Le Garrec in February 1921. Two years earlier, in 1919, Dufresne had signed an exclusive contract with Galerie Sagot-Le Garrec, which published his prints during the 1920s. These all carry the publisher's blindstamp: *Ed-Sagot-Editeur-Paris.*

46 *Sortie de bain*
After bathing, about 1920
Engraving with rocker tool and drypoint
on cream laid paper. Signed on the plate.
Signed, titled and numbered *13/40* in
pencil, with publisher's blindstamp.
322 x 307mm. Dufresne 31.
1994-5-15-5

Memories of North Africa emerged in
Dufresne's prints following his return to
Paris after living in Algeria from 1910 to
1912. The nudes shown here are related to
black African sculpture which Dufresne
hunted out in the flea markets of Paris. In
the manner of making a mezzotint,
Dufresne has taken the unusual step of
engraving this print with a rocker. The
highlights around the black seated figure
and the attendant drying her feet have been
achieved by scraping back the plate. Made
in about 1920, this print was later
published by Galerie Sagot-Le Garrec in
1923 in an edition of 40. This impression
formerly belonged to the Paris dealer Henri
Petiet, who also championed Dufresne's
prints between the wars.

47 *Une escale au Brésil*
Port of call in Brazil, about 1920
Etching, engraving and drypoint on
paper watermarked 'Alfred Porcaboeuf'.
Signed on the plate. Signed, titled and
numbered *1/25* in pencil, with publisher's
blindstamp. 230 x 300mm. Dufresne 35.
1949-4-11-2444
Bequeathed by Campbell Dodgson

Dufresne's initial training as a medal
engraver, first with Hubert Ponscarme and
then with Alexandre Charpentier, may
explain his unusual technical virtuosity.
By employing different tools and intaglio
techniques Dufresne creates a variety of
textures on the plate; here, for example, he
has punched dots to create tone on the two
nudes and hatched engraved lines for the
serving-maid's dress. Many of Dufresne's
etchings from this period were printed by
Alfred Porcaboeuf; his name is sometimes
found as a watermark on the paper for
Sagot-Le Garrec's editions. Campbell
Dodgson bought this impression from the
publisher in 1921, together with two other
Dufresne prints, now in the British
Museum.

48 *Le Banjo*
The banjo, about 1921
Etching and drypoint on cream laid
paper. Signed on the plate. Signed, titled
and numbered *7/20* in pencil, with
publisher's blindstamp. 240 x 327mm.
Dufresne 38.
1994-5-15-6

The carefree tropics are again suggested in
this etching. Occupying two separate zones
of the composition, a black musician,
dressed formally, plays to a naked woman
reclining on a hammock, although their
gaze is to the viewer, not to each other.
Published by Sagot-Le Garrec in 1923, this
print is sometimes also titled *Musique
nègre* or *La Guitare*.

49 *En escale*
Port of call, about 1922
Etching and drypoint. Signed on the
plate. Signed, titled and numbered *24/40*
in pencil, with publisher's blindstamp.
182 x 243mm. Dufresne 42.
1993-6-20-14

This was published by Sagot-Le Garrec in
1924. The sailor's port of call was a
common theme in the work of Dufresne and
his contemporary André Lhote during this
period.

Henri Laurens
1885-1954

A close friend of Braque from 1911,
Laurens was recognised as a leading
Cubist sculptor by 1915. While his first
prints date from this year, Laurens began
to concentrate on etching in 1921. He was
much encouraged by Kahnweiler who
published his etchings on returning to
France in 1920 when he opened Galerie
Simon.

50 *La Table*
The table, 1921
Etching on heavy wove paper. Signed
with initials on the plate. Signed and
numbered *23* in pencil. 174 x 222mm.
Völker 8.
1949-4-11-2506
Bequeathed by Campbell Dodgson

Strongly influenced by the Cubist still lifes
of Braque and Juan Gris, this etching
shows a guitar and sheet music placed on a
pedestal table. This impression was
purchased by Campbell Dodgson from the
London Gallery in 1937 for 2 guineas.

51 *Deux nues*
Two nudes, about 1929
Etching on thin laid paper. Signed and
numbered *15/50* in pencil. 197 x 269mm.
Völker 12.
1993-5-9-3

This is based on a terracotta sculpture
entitled *Deux femmes* which Laurens
made in about 1926. The volume and
massiveness of the figures recall the Art
Deco style which spread a diluted and
decorative form of Cubism from the mid-
1920s. Another etching of *Deux femmes*
also derives from his sculpture.

Jean Lurçat
1892-1966

52   *Odalisque*, about 1929
      Drypoint on cream laid paper. Signed on
      the plate. Signed and numbered *7/15* in
      pencil. 252 x 323mm.
      1946-12-14-2
      Presented by the Contemporary Art
      Society

Lurçat's first drypoints were made from the
mid-1920s. The subject of this print may
relate to Lurçat's extensive travels in North
Africa and the Middle East between 1924
and 1929. Equally it may have been inspired
by the fashionable success of the odalisque
theme in Matisse's lithographs (see
catalogue numbers 68 and 72) and
paintings of the early 1920s. Much of
Lurçat's work in printmaking was for book
illustration, while from the late 1930s he
became chiefly known as a tapestry
designer and maker.

Jacques Villon
1875-1963

53   *Baudelaire, au socle*
      Baudelaire, on a pedestal, 1920
      Etching on cream laid paper. Signed on
      the plate. Signed and numbered *4* in
      pencil. 417 x 281mm. Ginestet and
      Pouillon E.290.
      1949-4-11-2711
      Bequeathed by Campbell Dodgson

Sculpture played an important role in the
work of Villon. This etching is after a bust
of Baudelaire which his brother, Raymond
Duchamp-Villon, carved from wood in 1911.
The bust was often the starting point for
discussions on modern sculpture among
the Section d'Or Cubists, including Gleizes,
Archipenko and Marcel Duchamp, who met
at Villon's studio in Puteaux outside Paris
between 1911 and 1913. The etching shown
here was his first print since 1914 and
shows the way Villon indicated Cubist form
by etching ruled lines in different
directions. Campbell Dodgson formed a
large collection of Villon's etchings of the
1920s and 30s (see catalogue numbers 87
and 88), which came to the British Museum
as part of his bequest in 1949.
Unfortunately no example of Villon's
important Cubist printmaking before the
First World War was included. This print is
one of three etchings which Dodgson
purchased directly from Villon in 1937.

Pablo Picasso
Sculpteur et modèle agenouillé
Sculptor with kneeling model
1933 (catalogue number 55)
© Succession Picasso/DACS 1997

A return to classical order characterises the work of Picasso and Matisse in the post-war period. The multiple viewpoints and spatial complexities of Picasso's Cubism gave way to a neo-classical manner which emphasised the drawn line. Picasso's encounter with classical antiquity during a visit to Rome, Naples and Pompeii in 1917 largely led to this change in style and the adoption of classical subject matter in his art. Picasso's neo-classicism, with its spare, lucid line, is most apparent in the etched illustrations to Ovid's *Métamorphoses* (published in 1931) and in many of the plates from the *Vollard Suite* (catalogue numbers 55-9) produced between 1930 and 1936. The darker side of Picasso's psyche is explored through the metaphor of the classical Minotaur (catalogue numbers 58-60) in the 1930s. It was during this period that Picasso established a long-term creative relationship at the atelier of Roger Lacourière, where he made etchings and aquatints until the early 1950s. Picasso's lithographs produced in Mourlot's workshop from November 1945 are also in this section (catalogue numbers 63-7).

Matisse's work after the First World War likewise experienced a change in style. In 1917 he moved to Nice where he was based for the next ten years. The exotic theme of the odalisque, recalling the 19th-century neo-classicism of Ingres, began to dominate his paintings and lithographs from the early 1920s. But, unlike his earlier lithographs, the prints of this period show a greater emphasis on tonal drawing than on line. Matisse's interest in line returns in his etchings of 1929 and in his linocuts of the late 1930s, most notably in the 18 linocut illustrations to the classically inspired book *Pasiphaé*. Classical themes and an emphasis on drawing from classical models characterise the work of many other artists in the post-war period, as shown here in the prints of Derain and Galanis.

Pablo Picasso
1881-1973

54 *Deux femmes regardant un
modèle nu*
**Two women looking at a nude
model**, 1923
Drypoint, scraper and etching on
Montval laid paper. 6th state. Signed and
numbered *86/100* in pencil. 175 x 128mm.
Bloch 57; Baer 102.VIa.
1934-12-8-127
Presented by the Contemporary Art
Society

In the early 1920s Picasso often turned to
the classical theme of the Three Graces or
Three Women. Working on this plate in
autumn 1923, Picasso first drew the figures
in drypoint and then worked over the plate
with acid to obtain a grainy texture. He
then scraped parts of the plate to retrieve
the highlights. It was printed by Leblanc
and Trautmann in an edition of 100 for the
publisher Marcel Guiot in 1929. Acting on
behalf of the Contemporary Art Society,
Campbell Dodgson purchased this
impression in Paris, the year after it was
published; the purchase price then was
1,300 francs (£10.10s). In 1934, it was
presented by the Contemporary Art Society
to the British Museum.

55 *Sculpteur et modèle agenouillé*
Sculptor with kneeling model,
1933
Etching on laid Montval paper
watermarked Montgolfier. Dated on the
plate: *Paris 8 avril XXXIII*. Signed in
pencil. 368 x 298mm. Bloch 178;
Baer 331.Bc.
1979-7-21-66

This, together with catalogue numbers 56-
59, is from the famous *Vollard Suite* of 100
plates, the highpoint of Picasso's neo-
classical manner. In 1937 the dealer and
publisher Vollard selected 97 plates from a
larger group which Picasso had produced
in the course of seven years, from 1930 to
1936. This was in exchange for some
pictures that Picasso wanted. Vollard's
selection was rounded up to 100 with the
addition of three portraits of the dealer
himself (catalogue number 56). The 100
plates were printed by Lacourière in 1939
as follows: three suites on parchment; 50 on
laid Montval paper with large margins
watermaked *Montgolfier*; 250 on the same
paper with narrow margins watermarked
Picasso or *Vollard*. This impression is from
the suite of 50 on larger paper.

A major theme of the *Vollard Suite* is the
Sculptor's Studio, which is represented in
46 plates, almost half the series. Of these an
astonishing 40, including this print, were
produced between 20 March and 5 May
1933. Three years earlier Picasso bought
the château Boisgeloup near Gisors, forty
miles north-east of Paris, where he devoted
himself principally to making sculpture in
the following years. The model of this
period was Marie-Thérèse Walter who
became Picasso's lover in 1927, when she
was 17. A haunting presence in the *Vollard
Suite*, she appears here gazing in a mirror
propped against the artist's sculpted head
creased with age.

56 *Portrait of Vollard II*, 1937
Aquatint on laid Montval paper
watermarked: *Picasso*. Signed in red
crayon. 348 x 247mm. Bloch 231;
Baer 618.Bd.
1981-6-20-18

One of Picasso's greatest portraits, this is
one of three plates of Vollard which he
made in one day, 4 March 1937. Showing an
astonishing mastery of sugar aquatint, the
wily dealer's features are brushed in with
expressive economy. Although printed by
Lacourière before Vollard's death in a car
crash in July 1939, the great majority of the
edition for the *Vollard Suite* was not
released until after the Second World War
when 97 plates were bought by the dealer
Henri Petiet. The plates of the three
Vollard portraits were bought by Marcel
Lecomte, another Paris dealer, to the
intense annoyance of Petiet, who was
compelled to buy impressions from his
business rival in order to make up the
complete suite of 100.

57 *Sculpteur et son modèle avec la
tête sculptée du modèle*
**Sculptor and model with
sculpted head of model**, 1933
Etching on laid Montval paper with
Montgolfier watermark. Dated on the
plate: *Paris 2 avril XXXIII*. Signed in
pencil. 193 x 267mm. Bloch 171;
Baer 324.Bc.
1979-7-21-65

This is another plate from the *Vollard
Suite* on the theme of the Sculptor's Studio.
It is one of four etchings Picasso made in
the space of three days showing the
sculptor and his model resting together in
the studio; before them is a Boisgeloup
head, whose prominent profile is based on
Marie-Thérèse's features. Both sculptor
and model are crowned with an ivy wreath.

58 *Scène bacchique au minotaure*
Bacchic scene with minotaur,
1933
Etching on laid Montval paper with
Montgolfier watermark. Dated on the
plate: *Paris 18 mai XXXIII*. Signed in
pencil. 298 x 367mm. Bloch 192;
Baer 351.IIIBc.
1979-6-23-57

Both this etching and catalogue number 59
deal with the Minotaur theme, found in 15
plates of the *Vollard Suite*. Taking this idea
from classical mythology, Picasso
developed it as a personal metaphor in his
art. Half-man, half-beast, the Minotaur
made its first appearance in his etchings in
April 1933. Here its bestial side is revealed
in this depiction of a Bacchic orgy where
the Minotaur appears to be toasting the
artist's sexual conquests.

59 *Minotaure caressant une
dormeuse*
**Minotaur caressing a sleeping
woman**, 1933
Drypoint on laid Montval paper with
Montgolfier watermark. Dated on the
plate: *Boisgeloup 18 juinXXXIII*. Signed
in pencil. 297 x 367mm. Bloch 201;
Baer 369.IIBc.
1979-7-21-67

Crouching over the sleeping woman, the
Minotaur in this print is both a brutal
presence and a tender lover, showing the
two sides of his nature.

60 *Femme torero*
Woman bullfighter, 1934
Etching on laid Montval paper. Dated on
the plate: *Paris mardi 12 juin XXXIV.*
498 x 694mm. Bloch 1329; Baer 425.C.
1980-11-8-8

Here the Minotaur theme is transposed to
a bullfight. The ritual struggle of death
between bull and female bullfighter is
transformed to a personal one between
Picasso and Marie-Thérèse. Struggling
with the beautiful young torero, the
Minotaur bull attempts to deliver a final
kiss (or kiss of death) with his bestial lips.
About 50 impressions of this print and of
La Grande Corrida (catalogue number 61)
were printed in April 1939 just before
Vollard's death. Neither print was
published in a formal edition nor were any
impressions signed by Picasso. They only
appeared on the market after the artist's
death in 1973.

61 *La Grande Corrida, avec femme
torero*
**Large bullfight with woman
bullfighter**, 1934
Etching on laid Montval paper. Dated on
the plate: *Boisgeloup 8 septembre XXXIV.*
496 x 692mm. Bloch 1330; Baer 433.C.
1980-11-8-9

It is difficult to distinguish the elements
that make up this composition. The main
protagonists, bull, female bullfighter and
picador, are shown in a struggle to the
death. The spectators of this nightmarish
scene are shown behind the barrier in tiny
scale while Marie-Thérèse, depicted with
her characteristic profile upper right,
looks on with detachment at the deadly
fray taking place below.

62 *Tête de femme no. 7: Portrait de
Dora Maar*
**Head of woman no. 7: Portrait
of Dora Maar**, 1939
Colour drypoint before steel-facing on
laid Montval paper watermarked:
Picasso. 297 x 237mm. Bloch 1336;
Baer 655.Ba.
1994-10-2-7

Picasso began his liaison with Dora Maar,
a talented photographer, in May 1936. Part
of the Surrealist group with the poet Paul
Eluard (see catalogue number 109), Man
Ray and the critic Roland Penrose, Dora
Maar has usually been identified as the
'weeping woman' in Picasso's series of
paintings from 1937, one of which is in the
Tate Gallery. In printmaking Picasso made
seven portraits of Dora Maar, mostly
colour aquatints with Lacourière in the
first half of 1939, however this was the the
only portrait executed entirely in drypoint.
Four plates were used, one for each colour,
starting with pink, blue, brown and finally
black. Picasso used emery paper to rub the
tonal areas of Dora Maar's severely
distorted face. Her hair, executed in
delicate threads of drypoint, is particularly
visible in this impression. It is one of seven
proofs pulled by Lacourière before the
plate was steel-faced for an edition of 105.
The edition was never numbered or signed;
it was retained by Picasso until his death.

63 *Les deux femmes nues*
Two nude women, 1945
Lithograph on woves Arches paper. 13th
state. 266 x 360mm. Mourlot 16.XIII.
1990-4-7-14
Presented by Dr Frederick Mulder

Picasso had not made lithographs for some
fifteen years but in November 1945 he
began a four month period of intense
experimentation at Mourlot's lithographic
workshop in the rue de Chabrol. As
Fernand Mourlot relates in his catalogue
of Picasso's lithographs:

' (he) scarcely left the premises for four
months. He would come in at 9 o'clock in
the morning and work continuously until
late at night, often after 8pm.'

 Jean Célestin, who worked closely beside
Picasso at Mourlot's, later recalled:

'We gave him a stone and, two minutes later
he was at work with crayon and brush. And
there was no stopping him. As
lithographers we were astonished by him.
When you make a lithograph, the stone has
been prepared, and if you have to make a
correction the stone has to be re-touched.
...Right. We run off 12 to 15 proofs for him
and return the stone to him in good order.
Then he makes his second state. ...And he
would scrape and add ink and crayon and
change everything! After this sort of
treatment the design generally becomes
indecipherable and is destroyed. But, with
him! Each time it would turn out very well.
Why? That's a mystery.' (cited in Fernand
Mourlot, *Picasso Lithographs*, Paris: André
Sauret-Les Editions du Livre, 1970, n.p.)

This lithograph went through at least
eighteen different states. Shown here is a
proof of the thirteenth state and one from
the final state (catalogue number 64). The
subject of two women together in a
bedroom, one asleep, the other awake,
became an important theme for Picasso; it
is seen again, for example, in the later
linocuts (catalogue numbers 158-9). The
woman seated at left resembles Françoise
Gilot whom Picasso first met in May 1943,
although she only began to feature in his
work in 1945.

64 *Les deux femmes nues*
Two nude women, 1945
Lithograph on wove Arches paper. Final
state. 317 x 425mm. Mourlot 16.XVIII.
1990-4-7-15

This final state was published in a signed
and numbered edition of 50. The head of
Françoise Gilot is now transformed into an
abstracted bird-like form. Light-hearted
sketches of insects and birds decorate the
margins.

65 *David and Bathsheba*, 1947
Lithograph on wove paper. 2nd state.
Dated on the zinc plate: *30 mars 1947*.
Signed and numbered *44/50* in pencil. 644
x 490mm. Bloch 440; Mourlot 109.II.
1966-7-23-4
Presented by Mrs Basil Gray

The subject of King David secretly
watching Bathsheba being bathed by her
attendants is based on a painting by
Cranach in Berlin. Picasso transformed his
image through ten different states,
progressing from black marks made on a
light ground to white lines on a black
ground. This progression is shown here in
an early second state made in March 1947
and a later eighth state (catalogue number
66) of two years later, in April 1949.

66 *David and Bathsheba*, 1947- 49
Lithograph on wove paper. 8th state.
655 x 488mm. Mourlot 109.VIII.
1995-6-18-27

This proof of the eighth state formerly
belonged to the printer Gaston Tutin, with
whom Picasso worked at Atelier Mourlot.
It was made on 10 April 1949. Two days
later, on 12 April 1949, Picasso made a
complete change and removed everything
from the zinc lithographic plate, leaving
the design only as engraved grooves, which
were then re-drawn with lithographic pen.

67 *Figure noire*
Black figure, 1948
Lithograph on wove paper. 643 x 498mm.
Mourlot 126.
1996-9-29-4

Like catalogue number 66, this also
belonged to the printer Gaston Tutin. It
was made at Mourlot's workshop on 20
November 1948 and printed in an edition of
50. The design was worked out of the flat
black of lithographic ink with sandpaper in
the area of the face and with a needle for
the outline. The ear, neck and lower part of
the bodice were left in reserve as areas of
white on the zinc plate and then worked on
with crayon.

Henri Matisse
1869-1954

68 *Le Repos du modèle*
Resting model, 1922
Lithograph on greyish chine volant.
Signed on the stone. Signed in pencil. 222
x 304mm. Duthuit 416.
1949-4-11-3347
Bequeathed by Campbell Dodgson

At the end of 1917 Matisse moved to Nice
where for the next decade he painted
numerous odalisques and nudes which
became fashionable among collectors of the
period. This print marks Matisse's return
to lithography after his last serious
interest in the technique in 1913. He was
persuaded to take up lithography again by
the print dealer and publisher Edmond
Frapier, who ran the Galerie des Peintres-
graveurs, at 32 rue Victor-Massé, in
Montmartre. This print comes from a
deluxe edition of about 85; a larger,
ordinary edition of 525 unsigned
impressions was included among the
sixteen lithographs by various painters
represented in Frapier's *Album des
peintres-lithographes de Manet à Matisse*
issued about 1925.

Between 1922 and 1929, Matisse made a key
group of lithographs, many of them of the
odalisque. Unlike the earlier series of 1906
(catalogue numbers 5-7) and 1913
(catalogue number 8), these prints rely
heavily on shading and modelling for a
more realistic depiction of the nude. They
were mostly printed at the Atelier
Duchâtel, the lithographic workshop used
for Frapier's publications (see catalogue
numbers 80-3).

69 *La Robe d'organdi*
The organdie dress, 1922
Lithograph on greyish chine volant.
Signed and numbered *13/50* in ink. 425 x
278mm. Duthuit 423.
1940-4-13-33
Bequeathed by Mr Frank Hindley Smith

The model's demure formal pose in this
lithograph derives from paintings of the
early 1920s where she is seated in an
interior. The simplicity of her dress is
counterpointed by the arabesques
decorating the wall behind her.

70 *Arabesque*, 1924
Lithograph on greyish chine volant.
Signed and numbered *48/50* in pencil. 486
x 320mm. Duthuit 449.
1949-4-11-3350
Bequeathed by Campbell Dodgson

Here the arabesque patterns seem to
enwrap the model. Matisse later explained
their function in his drawing:

'The jewels or the arabesques never
overwhelm my drawings from the model,
because these jewels and arabesques form
part of my orchestration. Well placed, they
suggest the form or the value accents
necessary to the composition of the
drawing.' (Matisse, 'Notes of a Painter on
his Drawing' (1939) in Flam 1995, p. 131)

71 *Nu au coussin bleu*
Nude with blue cushion, 1924
Lithograph on Arches wove paper. Signed
and numbered *24/50* in pencil. 615 x
475mm. Duthuit 442.
1926-3-13-186
Presented by the Contemporary Art
Society

The model was Henriette Darricarrère, a
local girl from Nice, who had a flair for
play-acting Matisse's fantasy of the
odalisque. Matisse, who employed her from
1920 to 1927, later wrote:

'My models, human figures, are never just
"extras" in an interior. They are the
principal theme of my work. I depend
absolutely on my model, whom I observe at
liberty, and then I decide on the pose which
best suits *her nature* ... then I become a
slave of that pose.' (Matisse, 'Notes of a
Painter on his Drawing' (1939) in Flam
1995, p. 131)

Fascinated by this pose of the model seated
with arms raised above her head and one
leg raised, Matisse also used it in a closely
related painting of the same title, also
executed in 1924, and in another lithograph
of the same composition made a year later,
where the armchair is draped with a floral
pattern. It also appeared in a bronze
sculpture *Grand nu assis* (Minneapolis
Institute of Arts, Minneapolis), made in
1925. On behalf of the Contemporary Art
Society, Campbell Dodgson bought this
impression in June 1925 for £4 from Galerie
Bernheim-Jeune in Paris, which was
Matisse's contracted dealer from 1917 until
1926. The principal outlet for viewing the
most recent work produced in Nice, it was
to Bernheim-Jeune that nearly every
collector, including the Americans Albert
Barnes and Claribel Cone, came to buy
their Matisse.

72 *Grande odalisque à la culotte bayadère*
Large odalisque in striped pantaloons, 1925
Lithograph on thin greyish laid paper. Signed and numbered *39/50* in pencil. 542 x 438mm. Duthuit 455.
1932-5-14-65
Presented by the Contemporary Art Society

Wearing only exotic striped trousers, Matisse's model in the studio is transformed into this voluptuous odalisque of the harem. Here Matisse comes closest in spirit to the exoticism of Ingres' Turkish bathers. Not unlike a charcoal drawing, the rich tonal effects in this lithograph contribute to the pose's sensuality. Today perhaps the most sought-after print by Matisse, Dodgson puchased this impression on behalf of the Contemporary Art Society for £5 in 1925, the year it was published.

73 *Nu allongé, les jambes repliées, avec un collier*
Nude lying down with legs crossed, wearing a necklace, 1929
Etching on greyish chine collé mounted on white wove paper. Signed and inscribed: *Essai* in pencil. 129 x 178mm. Duthuit 113.
1949-4-11-2573
Bequeathed by Campbell Dodgson

In 1929 Matisse largely stopped painting and devoted the year to making a group of more than 100 etchings and drypoints. These were nearly all nudes, sometimes in a seemingly classical pose as shown here, where the figure's pose recalls that of a bucolic piper. This is one of two recorded trial proofs outside the edition of 25. Another version of this pose without the necklace was also etched at this time.

74 *Nu renversée*
Nude upside down, 1931
Etching on wove paper. Signed and numbered *25/25* in pencil. 242 x 178mm. Duthuit 228.
1994-5-15-8

In this unusual pose the model is placed upside down; the etching is misleadingly described and reproduced the other way round in Duthuit's catalogue raisonné. Matisse usually had his etchings printed on a chine collé to create a flat background tone. But in this etching a film of ink has been left on the plate to provide a delicate grey tone.

75 *Nu au bracelet*
Nude with bracelet, 1940
Linocut. 244 x 178mm. Duthuit 725. On loan from the Hunterian Art Gallery, University of Glasgow. Acc. no. 21180

Taking up the linocut in 1938 when he produced almost 30 prints, Matisse wrote eloquently of the particular qualities obtained from linoleum:

'I have often thought that this simple medium is comparable to the violin with its bow: a surface, a gouge - four taut strings and a swatch of hair. The gouge, like the violin bow, is in direct rapport with the feelings of the engraver. And it is so true that the slightest distraction in the drawing of a line causes a slight involuntary pressure of the fingers on the gouge and has an adverse effect on the line. Likewise, a change in the pressure of the fingers that hold the bow of a violin is sufficient to change the character of the sound from soft to loud.' (Matisse, 'How I made my Books' (1946) in Flam 1995, p. 168.)

This example, cut in 1940, is from the unnumbered edition published by the Chalcographie of the Louvre which carry a printed signature. Matisse's interest in the technique culminated in the eighteen linocuts produced for Montherlant's book, *Pasiphaé*, published by Fabiani in Paris in 1944, a copy of which is in the Victoria & Albert Museum's National Art Library.

Demetrius Galanis
1879-1966

76   ***The Three Graces**, 1923*
Wood-engraving on heavy japan paper.
Signed and numbered *1/8* in pencil.
452 x 358mm.
1949-4-11-4580
Bequeathed by Campbell Dodgson

Classical bathers and the theme of the
Three Graces often occur in Galanis' work
of the 1920s. Of particular importance to
this Greek-born artist, who arrived in Paris
in 1900, was the work of Raphael and the
engravings of Marcantonio Raimondi
which he would have seen during the
Raphael 400-year celebrations in Paris in
1920.

The British Museum also owns an early
state of this print in which only the bather
at right has been engraved; the rest of the
block is printed solid black. Galanis, who
also made mezzotints, seems to have been
much influenced by the mezzotint
technique in the way he worked the
highlights out of the black in this wood-
engraving. With the multiple tool,
originally used by 19th-century
reproductive engravers, he was able to
engrave several parallel lines at the same
time. Galanis' method was introduced
about 1923 by his American pupil Marion
Mitchell to Leon Underwood's school in
London, where it made a strong impact on
the more unconventional wood-engravings
produced by Blair Hughes Stanton and
Gertrude Hermes during the 1930s.

77   *Nue*
Nude, 1927
Etching on Arches wove paper. Signed on
the plate. Signed and numbered *79/150* in
pencil. 450 x 316mm.
On loan from the Hunterian Art Gallery,
University of Glasgow. Acc. no. Add 353
(2756b)

Like Laboureur (see catalogue number 24),
Galanis made a special study of 15th and
16th-century prints. This etching comes
from *Le Chien de Pique*, an album of
modern prints published by Au Sans Pareil
in June 1927. Galanis' highly individual use
of hatching to model form derives from his
close study of the Mannerist engravings of
Goltzius and other late 16th-century Dutch
engravers.

André Derain
1880-1954

78   *Bust of young woman smoothing her hair*, 1927
Plate 11 from the suite *Métamorphoses*
Lithograph on wove paper. Signed,
numbered *78/100* and annotated: *11* in
pencil. 451 x 364mm. Adhémar 71.
1932-5-14-64
Presented by the Contemporary Art
Society

Métamorphoses was a suite of twelve
lithographs comprising Derain's studies of
women, shown of head or bust length. It
was published in an edition of 100 by
Editions des Quatre Chemins in 1927, at
the height of Derain's popularity. The suite
contains a variety of drawing styles.
Particularly noticeable here is the heavy
working of the hair. The same model
appears in another lithograph within the
album, in which her dark hair is plaited
and coiled into a tight chignon. This
impression was purchased by Dodgson on
behalf of the Contemporary Art Society for
£3.16s.6 from the print dealer Petiet in
November 1929.

79   *Torse de femme*
Woman's torso, about 1927
Lithograph on wove paper. Signed and
inscribed: *Tirée à 25 épreuves; no. 13* in
pencil. 460 x 340mm. Adhémar 74.
1930-1-18-32
Presented by Campbell Dodgson

Derain made numerous drawings of the
female torso between 1925 and 1930, when
for long periods the model would be posed
almost daily. The sculptural modelling in
this lithograph is quite similar to the
classical torso drawings of his friend, the
sculptor Charles Despiau. Derain achieved
the delicate tonalities seen here by using
the broad edge of the lithographic crayon.
As Derain had his own press and litho
stones, it is quite possible that Petiet
bought from him the entire *tirage*, or
edition, which numbered 25 proofs, as
stated on this impression.

Jean-Emile Laboureur
L'Entomologiste
The entomologist
1932-33 (catalogue number 94)
© ADAGP, Paris and DACS, London 1997

The period between the wars in Paris saw the rise of the print dealers who were responsible for publishing the prints of both established and emerging artists to a wider market. Until his death in 1939 as the result of a car crash, Ambroise Vollard remained the dominant publisher for the leading avant-garde artists, notably Picasso (see Section 4). But he also commissioned Rouault (catalogue numbers 84-6) and other less prominent artists to make etchings and lithographs in the 1920s and 30s. Sometimes, as in the case of Rouault, these were printed but never published in Vollard's lifetime.

Edmond Frapier, who owned the Galerie des Peintres-graveurs in Montmartre, was more commercially minded. As well as Matisse (catalogue number 68), Frapier persuaded the older Nabis artists of the 1890s, Bonnard and Denis, to return to making lithographs for inclusion in his portfolios which he issued from 1925. The first was a mixed portfolio of sixteen lithographs entitled *Album des peintres-lithographes de Manet à Matisse*. This was followed by a series of seven albums entitled *Maîtres et petits maîtres d'aujourd'hui* which were devoted to individual artists, such as Rouault, Maillol and Vlaminck; these were published with accompanying essays in several languages, including Spanish and Japanese.

Whereas Frapier concentrated on publishing lithographs, the print dealer Henri Petiet supported a core group of etchers between the wars, including Goerg, Laboureur, Gromaire and De Segonzac. After Vollard's death most of his stock was bought by Petiet who became one of the most important dealers of modern prints in Paris after the Second World War.

Pierre Bonnard
1867-1947

80 *Le Bain*
The bath, about 1925
Lithograph printed in sanguine ink on
wove paper. Signed in pencil. 297 x
200mm. Bouvet 92a.I
1949-4-11-3171
Bequeathed by Campbell Dodgson

Madame Bonnard in her bath was a
favourite subject for the artist. This
lithograph was commissioned by the Paris
print publisher Edmond Frapier for his
*Album des peintres-lithographes de Manet à
Matisse* (the cover is shown in a nearby
table-case). Published in a very large
edition, there were 95 signed impressions
(including ten deluxe proofs printed in
sanguine, as shown here) and 575 for the
second state which carried a lithographed
signature. However, it appears most of the
edition was destroyed in the Second World
War when Frapier lost his stock during the
bombing of Royan, a coastal town near
Bordeaux, where the publisher had settled
after fleeing Occupied Paris.

81 *Femme debout dans sa
baignoire*
Woman standing in her bath,
1925
Lithograph on wove paper. Signed with
monogram on the stone. Signed and
numbered *7/100* in pencil. 295 x 193mm.
Bouvet 94.
1949-4-11-5045.1
Bequeathed by Campbell Dodgson

This is from a Bonnard album of four
lithographs which Frapier issued in 1925 as
part of a series entitled *Maîtres et petits
maîtres d'aujourd'hui*. Accompanying the
album was an essay by the critic Claude
Roger-Marx who had first supported
Bonnard and the Nabis artists in the 1890s.
Unlike Bonnard's earlier work, however,
the prints in the Frapier album are based
on compositions in his paintings. This
lithograph of Bonnard's wife depicted in
chiaroscuro against the pattern of the tiled
bathroom wall is after a painting of 1924.

82 *Paysage du Midi*
**Landscape in the South of
France**, 1925
Lithograph on wove paper. Signed with
monogram on the stone. Signed and
numbered *7/100* in pencil. 215 x 292mm.
Bouvet 95.
1949-4-11-5045.2
Bequeathed by Campbell Dodgson

This is a view of Le Cannet looking across
the bay of Cannes to the mountains of
Esterel. Bonnard first visited the town in
1922 and returned regularly each year,
eventually purchasing the Villa du Bosquet
in February 1926. Like catalogue number
81, this lithograph comes from Frapier's
Bonnard album of 1925 which was printed
by Atelier Duchâtel in an edition of 100 in
Paris; the publisher's blind stamp is found
on each impression.

Georges Rouault
1871-1958

83   *Parade*, 1926
> Lithograph on wove paper. Signed with monogram on the stone. Signed and numbered *7/100* in pencil. 317 x 264mm. Chapon and Rouault 319.
> 1949-4-11-5047.3
> Bequeathed by Campbell Dodgson

Rouault took up lithography in 1925 at the urging of the publisher Edmond Frapier who asked him to contribute a print to his *Album des peintres-lithographes de Manet à Matisse*. A year later, as part of his continuing series *Maîtres et petits maîtres d'aujourd'hui*, Frapier issued an album of four Rouault lithographs, which included the example shown here. Accompanying the Frapier album was an essay by Jacques Maritain, with parallel texts in German and English, the last provided by Campbell Dodgson. In all, Rouault made 35 lithographs for Frapier between 1925 and 1932; they were mostly drawn by Rouault on paper for transfer to the stone and printed at the Atelier Duchâtel. The subject of poorly paid circus performers preoccupied Rouault for over 40 years. In his text Maritain wrote of Rouault's work:

'... these women and clowns, these monstrous and miserable fleshly bodies, with their subdued harmonies ... express the wound of sin, the sadness of fallen nature ... Thus this pathetic art has a profoundly religious significance.'

84   *Automne*
Autumn, 1933
> Lithograph on thin brown Montval laid paper. 7th state. Signed with monogram, dated and titled on the stone. Signed and inscribed in ink: *7 état Automne*. 440 x 580mm. Chapon and Rouault 364.VII.
> 1994-7-24-1

This is the most ambitious of the four large lithographs that Rouault made for Vollard between 1926 and 1933. He first worked on this print in 1927 when Vollard published an edition of 30. Six years later, in 1933, Rouault returned to the stone and obsessively worked through a total of eleven states. Shown here is a proof of the seventh state printed on brown paper; it formerly belonged to Henri Petiet, the Paris print dealer and publisher. An edition of 60 was printed of the eighth state and a further 175 of the final state. All the proofing and printing of the various editions was done at Atelier Clot, where Rouault had tried out colour lithography with a single example in 1910. This composition, which recalls his studies of bathers of 1906-14, clearly haunted Rouault. After his intense labour on the **Automne** lithograph, Rouault repeated the composition in an equally large aquatint printed in fiery autumnal colours at Lacourière's atelier in 1936.

85 *Les Fleurs du mal*
Flowers of evil, 1933
Lithograph on greyish laid paper. Final
state. Signed with monogram and date on
the stone. 304 x 213mm. Chapon and
Rouault 365.IV.
1972-4-8-7

This was the last lithograph that Rouault
made. He appropriated the two central
figures from **Automne** (catalogue number
84) to another stone, making some
modifications to the composition. The title
of this print suggests that it may have been
a projected illustration to Charles
Baudelaire's poem. In all Rouault made
three series of illustrations to *Fleurs du
mal*. The first was a set of fourteen
aquatints made between 1926 and 1927
which, despite being printed in an edition
of 500, was never put on the market by the
publisher Vollard. A second series of 36
plates was made in photogravure of
uncertain date. Finally a suite of aquatints
was produced between 1936 and 1938.

86 *Le Condamné s'en est allé*
The condemned man has gone,
1930
Aquatint and photogravure. Signed and
dated on the plate. 492 x 337mm. Chapon
and Rouault 172.
1979-7-21-59
Presented by Antony Griffiths, Esq.

Conceived on the death of his father in
1912, Rouault's long drawn-out series
Miserere et Guerre, from which this plate
comes, has a complicated history. The
series was begun in 1916 but changes to the
plates during the 1920s and difficult
relations between Rouault and Vollard over
exactly which plates were to be included
meant that the final series was not
published until 1948, after Rouault had
won a lawsuit against Vollard's heirs. This
proof is one of 46 plates from the *Miserere*
series which were reworked at Maurice
Potin's atelier between 1928 and 1932 but
rejected from the final suite. It was
developed from a plate of the same title
made in 1922. Maurice Potin's atelier
specialised in aquatint and photogravures;
on the verso of this studio proof is a colour
aquatint by a different artist showing a
conventional view of a market town in
Normandy.

Jacques Villon
1875-1963

87 *Nu à genoux*
Kneeling nude, 1929
Etching and drypoint on laid paper.
Signed and dated on the plate. Signed
and inscribed: *épreuve d'artiste* in pencil.
223 x 164mm. Ginestet and
Pouillon E.328.
1949-4-11-2716
Bequeathed by Campbell Dodgson

This is from a group of etched studies of
the figure based on drawings of bathers by
the sea made in 1927. Villon drew the
initial outline of the nude in drypoint
before using a ruler to etch the regular
pattern of horizontal and vertical lines that
cover the plate. Pierre Courtin (catalogue
number 141), who as a young man acted as
Villon's assistant, recalls that Villon used
ferric perchloride rather than nitric acid to
bite the plate, thus ensuring a regularity in
the depth of the lines. This is an artist's
proof outside the published edition of 50.

88 *Le grand dessinateur assis*
The large seated draughtsman,
1935
Drypoint and etching on laid paper.
Signed and numbered *9/50* in pencil. 265 x
200mm. Ginestet and Pouillon E.385.
1949-4-11-2710
Bequeathed by Campbell Dodgson

The finest of Villon's self-portraits, this was
preceded by three oils, a much smaller
etching and two drawings. The artist is
shown seated at a tilted drafting table in
his studio. Behind him is a bronze by his
brother Raymond Duchamp-Villon
standing on a modelling pedestal. To the
left of the curtain is the barely discernible
Bust of Baudelaire, also by Raymond,
which had been the subject of two earlier
etchings by Villon in 1920 (see catalogue
number 53). The extreme chiaroscuro of
this self-portrait recalls the etchings of
Rembrandt which Villon greatly admired.

Jean Lurçat
1892-1966

89 *Four bathers*, about 1927-28
Drypoint on heavy wove paper. Signed on
the plate. Signed and numbered *126/160*
in pencil. 498 x 393mm.
1980-5-10-11

The large scale of this drypoint is unusual
among Lurçat's prints, which were mostly
destined for book illustration. Despite an
edition size of 160, next to nothing is
known about the circumstances of this
print's publication. The print relates to a
similar subject published by Cahiers d'Art
in 1928 as a drypoint illustration to
Philippe Soupault's monograph on Lurçat.
The surrealistic figures in both prints
share a certain affinity with Picasso's
bathers series of the late 1920s.

Jules Pascin
1885-1930

Born in Bulgaria as Julius Mordecai Pincas, the son of a wealthy grain merchant, he changed his name to Pascin at the request of his father after settling in Paris in 1905. Much of Pascin's subject matter drew upon his familarity with the brothels of Montmartre and Montparnasse. Celebrated during the 1920s as one of Paris's most bohemian artists, his dissolute and alcoholic life ended in suicide on 2 June 1930.

90 *Nègres en Floride*
   Blacks in Florida, 1928
   Soft-ground etching on Arches wove paper. Inscribed in pencil: *épreuve d'artiste/ approuvée par Pascin/ Nègres en Floride/ A Monsieur Campbell Dodgson/ Lucy Krohg/ 28-11-32.* 201 x 253mm.
   Hemin, Krohg, Perls and Rambert 148.
   1949-4-11-2588
   Bequeathed by Campbell Dodgson

Pascin revisited the United States in 1927 in order to keep his American citizenship which he had taken out in 1920 after spending the First World War years there. During his first stay he had produced a group of etchings and drypoints of Florida while travelling through the southern states of America and Cuba in 1917. This soft-ground etching, which resembles the effect of a pencil drawing, was an outcome of Pascin's second visit. Typically Pascin makes no social comment on the scene observed.

This etching is dedicated by Lucy Krohg, Pascin's former mistress, to Campbell Dodgson, then Keeper of Prints and Drawings at the British Museum. Lucy Krohg, wife of the Norwegian artist Per Krohg, became Pascin's mistress in 1920 and later joined him on his second visit to America. After Pascin's suicide his widow, the etcher Hermine David, and Lucy Krohg were made co-heirs of the estate; the Galerie Lucy Krohg, which opened shortly after Pascin's death, remained the main outlet for his work until the 1960s.

Edouard Goerg
1893-1969

Born in Sydney while his French father was there on business selling champagne, Goerg was brought up in Paris and encouraged to make prints by Laboureur whom he met in 1923. During the 1930s most of Goerg's etchings were published by the dealer Henri Petiet, who admired their extraordinary detail and imaginative power.

91 *Le Feu et l'eau à l'exposition 1937*
   Fire and water at the 1937 Exposition, 1937
   Etching on Rives wove paper. Signed with monogram on the plate. Signed, titled and numbered in pencil: *ép. d'artiste 2/15.* 446 x 297mm.
   1949-4-11-2470
   Bequeathed by Campbell Dodgson

This comes from an album of prints by various artists commissioned by the French Government. The album was intended to be offered to distinguished visitors to the 1937 World Exposition held in Paris. Here Goerg depicts a spectacular display of water fountains in the Seine coinciding with the explosion of fireworks from the top of the Eiffel Tower. This artist's proof was printed before the published edition of 100 which shows a dragonfly etched as a *remarque*, or little sketch, in the lower margin.

92   *Les oiseaux chassés du ciel*
      The birds hunted from the sky,
      1938
      Etching on wove paper. Signed, titled and
      numbered *11/70* in pencil. 296 x 448mm.
      1996-6-8-12

Goerg produced a series of large and
cataclysmic compositions in the years
preceding the outbreak of the Second
World War. A committed member of the
political left, he was profoundly affected by
the Civil War after his visit to Spain with
Louis Aragon in 1937. This large visionary
etching counts as Goerg's masterpiece:
here memories of the fantastic imagery of
Brueghel and Bosch, which he had seen on
an earlier visit to the Low Countries in
1934, are combined with the hallucinatory
horror provoked by Goerg's battle with
heroin addiction. This impression, which
comes from Petiet's edition of 70 published
in 1938, was later exhibited at the 1952
Venice Biennale.

93   *Les Poissons chassés de l'eau*
      The fish hunted from the water,
      1938-42
      Etching on wove paper. Titled in pencil.
      327 x 254mm.
      1996-6-8-18.
      Presented by Christian Germak, Esq.

This is a companion plate to catalogue
number 92. The fish and the birds flee their
natural elements: the fish appear in the sky
while the birds swarm into a chasm that
has opened up in the earth. Begun in the
same year as catalogue number 92, this
plate was finally published by Petiet in
1942. It is one of several prints by Goerg
recently presented by the artist's son-in-law
to the British Museum.

Jean-Emile Laboureur
1877-1943

94   *L'Entomologiste*
      The entomologist, 1932-33
      Engraving on wove paper. 4th state.
      Signed with monogram and dated on the
      plate. Signed and numbered *28/82* in
      pencil. 347 x 397mm. Laboureur 475.IV.
      1949-4-11-3109
      Bequeathed by Campbell Dodgson

A masterpiece of his late work, this large
and detailed plate took Laboureur more
than three months to engrave from October
1932 to January 1933. The plate buzzes with
life: sheltered beneath a rocky cliff lies a
veritable paradise crawling with insects
and filled with vegetation. The insects,
long grasses, brambles and oak-leaves are
described with precise detail in the
foreground. Like the amateur entomologist
with his magnifying glass, the viewer
becomes completely absorbed in finding
the insects inhabiting this corner of the
overgrown garden. This impression is from
an edition of 82 pulled of the fourth state
early in 1933. Laboureur then sold the plate
for 6,000 francs to the Chalcographie of the
Louvre in June 1933. Subsequent *tirages*, or
printings, have been taken periodically by
the Chalcographie.

Nina Negri
Capricorne
1954 (catalogue number 105)

Atelier 17 was the name of the famous printmaking workshop established by S. W. Hayter in Paris at 17 rue Campagne-Première in 1933. Hayter, who initially trained and worked as a chemist and geologist for an oil company in Iran, settled in Paris in 1926 where he met the Polish engraver Hecht, who encouraged him to take up engraving. In 1927 Hayter set up his print workshop. At Atelier 17 Hayter and his followers developed new methods of engraving which helped to spread Surrealist ideas of automatism and of the subconscious during the 1930s. Hayter's open personality, cosmopolitanism and philosophy of creative collaboration attracted a wide range of international artists to Atelier 17.

Before the outbreak of the Second World War Hayter left Paris and re-established Atelier 17 in New York where he brought the emigré European Surrealists in contact with the New York abstract expressionists (with the exception of catalogue number 108, this period is not covered in the present exhibition). In 1950 he returned permanently to Paris and reopened Atelier 17 at 278 rue de Vaugirard; it subsequently moved to different addresses. During the post-war years Atelier 17, under Hayter's direction, was much concerned with simultaneous colour printing and experiments in gestural mark making which coincided with the rise of Tachisme. Among his chief collaborators were the Chilean Zañartu and the Bombay-born Moti.

Stanley William Hayter 1901-1988 and Joseph Hecht 1891-1951

95 *La Noyée*
Drowned woman, 1946
Engraving on laid paper. 8th state. Signed by both artists, dated, titled and inscribed in pencil: *VIII état 1=1*. 346 x 443mm. Black and Moorhead 173.VIII.
1988-4-9-113

Unsettling in its drama and surrealistic imagery, this engraving is a collaboration between Hayter and Hecht who had formed a close artistic friendship during the 1930s at Atelier 17. From 1940 to 1949, Atelier 17 was based in New York and only returned to Paris in 1950. This print was made between July and August 1946 when Hayter, still based in New York, was visiting Paris and was determined to see his old friend Hecht make prints again after the separation of the Second World War. Both artists work in their own manner, making little adjustment to the other's style: Hayter engraved the two abstracted linear figures seen at top right and bottom left and another figure group on the horizon line; Hecht added the sphinx-like rock, the colony of cormorants and the dark wave patterns of the sea. It passed through ten different states before Hayter and Hecht started an edition of 50, which appears not to have been completed.

Roger Vieillard 1907-1989

A full-time research economist at a Paris bank until 1967, Vieillard devoted his evenings to making engravings, producing some 329 single-sheet prints as well as many engraved illustrations for *livres d'artiste* publications.

96 *Jacob et l'Ange*
Jacob and the angel, 1935
Engraving and soft-ground etching on laid paper. Signed in pencil. 241 x 253mm. Hacker 7.
1989-3-4-25

The surrealist imagery of this print, with its strange wooden stage placed in a desert landscape, drew the admiration of André Breton. In 1934, Hayter and Joseph Hecht at Atelier 17 showed Vieillard how to engrave deep lines onto the plate. Entitled ***Jacob and the angel***, the theme of this print has been described as a metaphor for the artist's struggle with the technique. The engraved figure of Jacob is similar to wire sculptures he was experimenting with at the time; the nebulous form of the angel is wittily etched in soft-ground. It is one of Vieillard's few prints to use more than one technique on the plate.

Dolf Rieser
1898-1983

Born in South Africa, Rieser first trained as an agricultural engineer in Zurich and then as a plant geneticist at Lausanne where he obtained his doctorate in 1922. Resolved to be a painter, he settled in Paris in 1928, where Hecht taught him to engrave. He absorbed Hayter's experiments with deep line-engraving and the use of different textures pressed onto the plate, at Atelier 17 during the 1930s.

97 ***Danse des guerriers cafres***
Kaffir war dance, 1938
Plate IX from the portfolio *Africa*. Engraving and soft-ground etching on laid Montval paper. Signed and numbered *64/100* in pencil. 207 x 287mm.
1986-10-4-51

This print comes from *Africa*, an album of ten engravings and etchings printed by Hecht at Atelier 17 in 1938. Evocative of Rieser's South African background, the album reveals his abiding interest in the art of the Kalahari bushmen and his scientific knowledge of plant life.

Oscar Dominguez
1906-1957

Dominguez, who arrived in Paris from the Canary Islands in 1927, joined the Surrealists in 1934 and took up their automatist methods. In 1935-36 he introduced his technique of *decalcomania,* whereby a sheet of paper was placed on top of another covered in gouache and the two then peeled apart. The results suggested imaginary landscapes or haunting dreamscapes.

98 ***Femme à bicyclette***
Woman with a bicycle, 1935
Etching with pencil additions on laid paper. 249 x 165mm.
1990-6-23-44

This enigmatic image is a working proof for a version of the frontispiece to Georges Hugnet's Surrealist poem, *La Hampe de l'imaginaire*, published by Editions G.L.M. in 1936. The conjunction of the nude and the bicycle shown here is pursued in Dominguez's *decalcomanie* of this period which often combine the motif of a lion with a bicycle. Made at Atelier 17, this print differs in some details, notably of the bird and the bicycle, from the published edition. In the final version there is no plate tone and the bicycle is reduced to a few spare lines uniting it more closely with the leaning figure.

Arpad Szenes
1897-1985

Born and trained in Budapest, Szenes arrived in Paris in 1925 where he soon became acquainted with Hayter. The prints he made at Atelier 17 between 1931 and 1939 reveal the spread of Surrealist ideas at the workshop. With the outbreak of war Szenes left Paris with his wife Vieira da Silva, the Portuguese painter and printmaker, for Portugal and then Brazil. Returning to Paris in 1947, Szenes did not take up printmaking again until 1968.

99 *Métamorphoses III*, 1935
Engraving, etching and soft-ground etching on laid paper. Signed, dated and numbered *1/30* in pencil. 237 x 178mm. 1994-7-24-7

In this print Szenes suggests the metamorphosis of leaves. The influence of Hayter is evident in the deeply engraved lines while the vegetal forms directly refer to Max Ernst's *Histoire naturelle*, an album of collotypes published in 1926 after his *frottage* drawings of 1925. Szenes' application of leaves and gauze on the soft-ground plate to obtain a variety of textures is a translation of Ernst's methods into intaglio printmaking.

Sigismund Kolos-Vari
born 1899

Like Szenes a year earlier, Kolos-Vari came from Hungary to Paris in 1926. Hélène Povolosky's gallery in the rue Bonaparte was a meeting place for young European artists in Paris, and was where Kolos-Vari met Jacques Lipchitz who brought him to Atelier 17. Already an accomplished printmaker before he left Hungary, Kolos-Vari quickly embraced Atelier 17's belief in the primacy of engraving. In 1934 he was included in the first exhibition of Atelier 17 artists in Paris. Both Kolos-Vari and Szenes became naturalised French citizens in the mid-1950s.

100 *Interior with seated nude and sleeping woman*, 1939
Engraving on wove Rives paper. Signed and dated in pencil. 205 x 280mm. 1994-5-15-20

This print shows Kolos-Vari's mastery of burin engraving to be the equal of Hecht and Vieillard. Playful allusions to Freudian dream symbolism are combined here with a pastiche of Picasso's etched depictions of Marie-Thérèse in the *Vollard Suite* (see catalogue numbers 55,57).

Enrique Zañartu
born 1921

Born in Paris of Chilean parents, Zañartu began to paint in Santiago, Chile in 1938. He first met Hayter in New York in 1943 where Atelier 17 had transferred for the duration of the Second World War. When Atelier 17 was re-established in Paris in 1950, Zañartu became Hayter's principal assistant in running the workshop. Speaking of Atelier 17 in his book *About Prints* (London: Oxford University Press, 1962, p. 92), Hayter wrote:

'It is directed by me personally, though the assistant director Zañartu knows as much about any of the processes as I do... .'

In the 1950s Zañartu made his name in Paris as a painter and printmaker working in the Tachiste style.

101   *Paysage fuyant*
      Fleeing landscape, 1959
      Engraving and aquatint printed in orange and dark green on wove Arches paper. Signed, dated, titled and numbered *13/50* in pencil. 310 x 242mm.
      1994-6-19-27

This is an example of Zañartu's gestural mark making in the Tachiste style. The sensitive marks of the burin in this plate are opposed by the heavier areas of open-biting, which have been filled in with orange aquatint. The directional wiping of the plate creates a fleeting horizon.

Nono Reinhold
born 1929

This Dutch-born artist studied in Amsterdam at the Rijksakademie before coming to Paris in 1952. In 1963, after ten years in Paris, she returned to live and work in Amsterdam.

102   *Composition bleu*
      Blue composition, 1953
      Engraving with scorper and aquatint printed in two shades of blue on wove paper. Signed, dated and inscribed: *épr. d'artiste* in pencil. Verso: titled in pencil. 87 x 139mm.
      1993-6-20-46

This print was made shortly after Reinhold started working at Atelier 17 in 1953. Like all her early Paris prints in which she experimented with colour, it is entirely abstract. Years later, in 1996, the artist wrote in a letter:

'Colour is essential in most of my prints. Often there is no association with reality: the intensity of colours gives another dimension to the expression in lines and surfaces.'

Reinhold has identified this print as a 'trial state' outside the edition of 50, although certainly no more than 35 were ever printed, all of them by her.

Raoul Ubac
1910-1985

Born in Belgium where he was brought up in the Ardennes, Ubac began living in Paris from 1930. He made contact with the Surrealists, participating in their events between 1934 and 1939, where he showed his collages and photographs, several of which were published in their review *Minotaure*. During this period he learnt to engrave with Hayter at Atelier 17.

103   *Untitled*, 1953
      Monotype in Prussian blue and black ink on heavy cream wove paper. Signed, dated and inscribed: *monotype* in pencil.
      583 x 475mm.
      1991-5-11-18

This monotype dates from Ubac's post-war period, when he had become fascinated with slate following his discovery of its possibilities as a surface in 1946. Instead of brushing ink on metal or glass in the conventional way for making a monotype, Ubac inked a piece of slate in dense black for this unique print. The shape of the stone suggested the mysterious baboon-like form looming out of midnight-blue depths.

Etienne Hajdu
born 1907

A Roumanian, born in Turda, Transylvania, Hajdu had studied at Budapest and then briefly with Hoffmann in Vienna, before arriving in Paris in 1927. From the early 1930s he began to make abstract sculptures. A close friend of Szenes (see catalogue number 99), he became acquainted with Hayter. But it was not until 1957 that he began to make his first inkless intaglio prints, which he called 'estampilles'.

104   *Untitled*, 1961
      Inkless intaglio on white handmade laid paper. Signed, dated and numbered *7/15*.
      340 x 230mm.
      1994-6-19-24

Made without ink at Atelier 17, this is very much a sculptor's print. Cut-out pieces of metal were arranged on the bed of the press and a sheet of heavy handmade paper placed on top before passing through the press and producing the embossed result. On Hajdu's technique, Hayter wrote in a revised edition of his *New Ways of Gravure* (New York: Watson Guptill Publications, 1981, p. 103):

'... the spaces between his elements are as important in the image as the actual surface indented by the plates, resulting in a relief in paper having sculptural form.'

Prefiguring the concerns of the Minimalist printmakers of the late 1960s and early 70s, Hajdu subtly plays on the contrast between the smooth surface of the indented areas and the uneven texture of the handmade paper.

Nina Negri
born 1909

Argentinian by birth, Negri studied in her native country and in Belgium and England, before settling in Paris where she made numerous engravings at Atelier 17 during the 1930s.

105 *Capricorne*, 1954
Engraving and aquatint in black, with colour printing in magenta and green, on wove paper. Signed, titled and inscribed; *épreuve d'artiste* in blue biro.
304 x 451mm.
1994-5-15-21

This is an example of Negri's colour prints which she began to produce from the early 1950s. Technically complex, it uses a mixture of intaglio techniques on the plate that characterise many of the prints made at Atelier 17 after the Second World War. The deeply engraved and aquatinted plate was inked through silkscreens for the colour, producing the clearly defined areas of magenta and green. Explaining this method of simultaneous colour printing in his book *About Prints* (1962, p. 62), Hayter remarked:

'... the colour has a freshness and brilliance impossible in multiple plate processes.'

This is an artist's proof outside the edition of 200 published by the Guilde Internationale de la Gravure in 1954.

Kaiko Moti
1921-1989

Born in Bombay of a Parsee family, Moti first came to England where he studied with Henry Moore at the Slade School in London. He settled in Paris in 1952 and worked closely with Hayter until 1955, becoming a chief assistant at Atelier 17. Like Krishna Reddy, a fellow Indian artist working at Atelier 17, Moti's work often refers to a mystical attitude to nature. He produced more than 200 prints during his 32-year association with Atelier 17.

106 *Abstract viscosity*, about 1953
Etching and aquatint with simultaneous colour printing on wove paper. Signed and inscribed: *Artist proof* in pencil.
350 x 246mm.
1988-10-1-39

In 1945, Hayter developed the technique of printing several colours simultaneously from a single plate by laying inks with different viscosities into the worked metal. It was a method which became widely used by artists at Atelier 17 from the late 1940s. In this example by Moti, aquatint was added to the 'wells' formed by the deep biting of the plate. Inks of different viscosities were rolled or wiped onto the plate: veils of green were created from layers of yellow ochre and cerulean blue, a favourite ink of Hayter's followers in the early 1950s. Also visible are traces of a red ink wiped into these areas. Aquatic biomorphic forms seem to be suggested here in this highly abstracted print. It is the work of a consummate colourist.

Pierre Alechinsky
born 1927

Born in Brussels, Alechinsky joined the Cobra group in 1949 with Corneille (see catalogue numbers 127-8). Settling in Paris in 1951, he took up a French government bursary to study engraving at Atelier 17 where he found that Hayter shared Cobra's interest in spontaneity and automatism.

107 *Haytérophilies*

A portfolio of 11 intaglio plates from 1952-53 published by Galerie La Hune in 1968. Each sheet signed and numbered *I/VI* in pencil. 407 x 577mm sheet.
1994-7-24-5.1-11

Shown here is plate 8 from a group of eleven intaglio prints published as a portfolio under the title *Haytérophilies* by Galerie La Hune, Paris in December 1968. Printed on the artist's own presses by the Atelier 17 printer Jean Clerté, these plates were originally produced in various small editions under the guidance of Hayter in 1952-53. This copy of the portfolio is one of six artist's proofs outside the published edition of 30. Alechinsky's affectionate dedication to his former teacher is amusingly drawn on the colophon. The intaglio plate shown here is concerned with spontaneous mark making, or 'taches', which preoccupied many of the gestural abstractionists of the 1950s. The poet Christian Dotrement provided the idea for this print where the writing is completely invented, the only legible words being those of the poet and the artist.

108 *Est ce qu'il neigeait?*
Is it snowing?, 1953

Etching and aquatint on wove paper. Signed on the plate. Signed, dated and numbered *16/50* in pencil. 345 x 248mm.
1987-4-11-10

First printed in Paris at Atelier 17 by Alechinsky, this etching incorporates a French text by Christian Dotremont in the body of the fabulous animal. The tachiste marks surrounding the beast owe their inspiration to Japanese calligraphy which Alechinsky learnt to write from 1952. The following year he published an article in the journal *Phases* on the relationship between Japanese calligraphy and the spontaneous drawing of certain Western artists. In 1954, the Chinese painter Walasse Ting, newly arrived in Paris, taught Alechinsky the Chinese manner of writing. These interests culminated in a trip to the Far East in 1955.

This impression comes from a portfolio entitled *21 Etchings and Poems* published in an edition of 50 by the Morris Gallery in New York. Begun in 1951 by Peter Grippe who took over Hayter's New York studio when Atelier 17 returned to Paris, this portfolio brought together artists and poets interested in creating 'pictured poems'. Most of the artists involved had worked at Atelier 17, either in Paris or in New York.

Alberto Magnelli
Untitled
1941 (catalogue number 118)
© ADAGP, Paris and DACS, London 1997

The rise of the dictators and the tragedy of the Spanish Civil War, which broke out in July 1936, provoked the political anger of artists, notably the Spanish exiles in Paris; Picasso, Gonzalez and Miró. The Spanish Republican Government invited Picasso and Miró to each make an enormous mural for the Spanish Pavilion at the World Exposition held in Paris in 1937. On 26 April 1937, German planes in support of Franco's regime bombed the Basque town of Guernica, annihilating most of the defenceless civilian population. *Guernica* became the theme of Picasso's contribution and the rallying cry of the Republican cause. It also motivated the completion of his savage denunciation of Franco in the comic strip etching ***Dream and lie of Franco*** (catalogue number 110).

Hayter's Atelier 17 harboured Spanish refugee artists and had considerable contact with the International Brigade. Two communal print projects aimed at raising support for the Republicans were *Solidarité* (catalogue number 109), produced in 1938, and *Fraternité* of 1939. Like Picasso, the Catalan Miró was greatly disturbed by the horror of the civil war in Spain, prompting him to make a series of prints of apocalyptic menace.

In Occupied France during the Second World War, the French artist Fautrier produced a group of prints on the theme of hostages (catalogue number 119) tortured by the Gestapo. Wartime restrictions on materials is poignantly evoked in Magnelli's woodcut (catalogue number 118) printed on a map of Grasse, the town where he had taken refuge.

109 *Solidarité*, 1938
A portfolio of seven intaglio prints by
seven artists printed at Atelier 17
accompanying a poem by Paul Eluard
with an English translation by Brian
Coffey and published by G.L.M., Paris,
April 1938
Each print signed and numbered *72/150*.
1949-4-11-5094.1-7
Bequeathed by Campbell Dodgson

Pablo Picasso 1881-1973
Woman's head with beret
Engraving with scraping, 105 x 75mm,
Baer 635c,
1949-4-11-5094.1

Joan Miró 1893-1983
Untitled
Etching and soft-ground etching, 100 x
80mm, Dupin 42,
1949-4-11-5094.2

Yves Tanguy 1900-1955
Untitled
Etching, 99 x 80mm, Wittrock 6,
1949-4-11-5094.3

André Masson 1896-1987
Untitled
Etching, 80 x 110mm, Saphire and
Cramer 12,
1949-4-11-5094.4

Initiated by Hayter as a communal effort at
Atelier 17, *Solidarité* was produced to aid
the children orphaned by the Spanish Civil
War. This small portfolio contained seven
intaglio prints contributed by seven artists
who supported the Republican cause: these
were Hayter, Dalla Husband and John
Buckland-Wright; the two Spaniards
Picasso and Miró; and two French
Surrealists, Masson and Tanguy. The
publisher Guy Lévis Mano (G.L.M), who
specialised in publishing the work of
Surrealist poets and artists in Paris, was
himself Spanish. He also acted as
distributor for the album: proceeds from
their sale went to the Spanish Republican
Children's Fund. Shown here are four
plates from the album, together with Paul
Eluard's poem 'Novembre 1936' and its
English translation by Brian Coffey.

Pablo Picasso
1881-1973

110 *Sueño y mentira de Franco*
Dream and lie of Franco, plates
1 and 2, 1937
Etching and aquatint on Montval laid
paper. Both plates dated at top: *8 janvier
1937*; plate 2 also dated below: *9 janvier
1937 - 7 juin 37*. Both sheets signed with
stamped signature and numbered *648/850*
in pencil. 318 x 422mm each. Bloch 297-98;
Baer 615-16.IIBe.
1980-11-8-10.1-2

Picasso began his comic strip satire of
Franco's pretensions to power in January
1937, where the dictator is caricatured as
an ugly polyp. However, the second plate
was only completed six months later, on 7
June 1937, after the bombing of Guernica.
These prints were available for sale in the
Spanish Pavilion at the 1937 World
Exposition in Paris, where Picasso's
Guernica was the centrepiece; proceeds
from their sale went to help the Republican
cause.

Julio Gonzalez
1876-1942

Born in Barcelona, where he first met Picasso, Gonzalez moved to Paris in 1900 although his sculpture only became better known from the late 1920s. *The Montserrat*, a major figurative piece inspired by the tragedy of the Spanish Civil War, was included in the 1937 World Exposition in Paris.

111 *Personnage*
Figure, about 1935
Drypoint. Signed and numbered *14/50* in pencil. 153 x 98mm.
On loan from the Hunterian Art Gallery, University of Glasgow. Acc. no. 21131

This drypoint is related to the constructivist metal sculptures Gonzalez was making with Picasso between 1929 and 1931. It comes from an album containing 23 prints by 23 different artists which was intended to serve as an *édition de luxe* for a book of essays on these artists and Marcel Duchamp to be published as *24 Essais* by Anatole Jakovski. Through lack of money, the essays were never published. But the album was printed in Paris by Editions G. Orobitz in an edition of 50: the first twenty sets were for sale and the remainder distributed among the artists and collaborators. Among the Paris avant-garde who participated were the Spanish contingent Picasso, Miró, Torrés-Garcia and the sculptor Gonzalez. Ben Nicholson, represented by an abstract woodcut which is in the British Museum's collection, was the only British artist among this international brigade. A complete album is kept in the National Art Library of the Victoria & Albert Museum.

Joan Miró
1893-1983

112 *Daphnis et Chloé*, 1933
Drypoint on heavy japan paper. Signed and dated in pencil: *11.33* . 260 x 325mm. Dupin 9.
On loan from the Hunterian Art Gallery, University of Glasgow. Acc. no. 18532

This is Miró's first single-sheet intaglio print. It was made in the etching studio of Marcoussis (see catalogue number 42), who taught him how to etch. Until 1939, most of Miró's etchings were made there, although the printing of the editions was handed to Lacourière at his atelier in Montmartre.

Printed in an edition of 100, this drypoint was commissioned by the Greek-born publisher Tériade who wanted a subject from classical mythology to support his newly launched review, *Minotaure*. The pastoral scene shows a shepherd playing his pipe before a dancing goat; the two distorted nudes on the horizon recall Picasso's bathers of the early 1930s. Miró first came to Paris at the end of 1918 after he had held his first solo exhibition in his native city of Barcelona.

113 *Aidez l'Espagne*
Help Spain, 1937
Colour stencil with Miró's offset
lithographed text below. 247 x 190mm
irreg. Dupin 17.
1981-6-20-44

On behalf of the people of Spain, a Catalan
farmer raises his hugely swollen fist in
defiance of Franco's Nationalists. It was
Miró's first political print and sold for 1
franc in aid of the Republican war effort.
Miró declares his frankly anti-fascist
position in the text below:

'In the present struggle I see, on the Fascist
side, spent forces; on the opposite side, the
people, whose boundless creative will gives
Spain an impetus which will astonish the
world.'

Printed in Paris at the Moderne
Imprimerie, there were two printings, one
without text. This comes from *Cahiers
d'Art*, nos 4-5, the art magazine of the Paris
avant-garde, which devoted a special issue
to the murals of Picasso and Miró at the
Spanish Republican Pavilion in the 1937
World Exposition held in Paris.

114 *Le Géante*
The giant, 1938
Drypoint on Arches wove paper. 351 x
239mm. Dupin 27.
1985-7-13-3

This is one of twenty etchings and
drypoints made in Marcoussis' studio and
published in editions of 30 in 1938. They
express Miró's anguish and horror at the
rise of fascism during the Thirties. Deeply
affected by the tragedy of the Spanish Civil
War and the looming threat of world war,
Miró presents an apocalyptic vision of
civilisation's impending collapse. Sharing
with Picasso a savage hatred of Franco,
Miró has created in this drypoint a rearing
monster who threatens to engulf the world.
As Dupin, Miró's cataloguer has observed,
these prints represent 'a desperate attempt
to exorcize the monsters by engraving their
features in the plate.'

115 *Plate XVII from the* **Barcelona
series**, 1944
Lithograph on wove paper. Signed, dated
and numbered *1/5* in pencil. 635 x 453mm.
Mourlot 22.
1984-5-12-8

116 *Plate XXXIV from the*
Barcelona series, 1944
Lithograph on wove paper. Signed, dated
and numbered *5/5* in pencil. 635 x 453mm.
Mourlot 39.
1984-5-12-10

Although Miró had made his first
lithograph on the stone in 1930, he was
indifferent to the technique until 1939
when Braque encouraged him to draw on
transfer paper. With the German invasion
of France, Miró fled to Spain in May 1940,
taking with him transfer paper and litho
crayons. This and catalogue number 116
are from a suite of 50 lithographs he drew
using these materials while living outside
Barcelona. Known as the *Barcelona series*,
they use Miró's graphic language of savage
distortion, squiggles and signs to evoke the
horrors of the Civil War. The series was
published in that city by Miró's Catalan
friend Joan Prats in 1944. As Mourlot, in
his catalogue raisonné of Miró's
lithographs, relates:

'In an old quarter of Barcelona, Prats
discovered a marvellous printer installed in
a tiny, ill-equipped shop ... The young
pressman, Mirallas, proved himself to be an
excellent workman and an expert at his
craft. He knew how to transfer Miró's
works onto stone correctly and how to pull
good proofs. The edition he made was
limited to five suites for sale, to pay for
himself, and two additional suites reserved
for the artist and Joan Prats ... the
publisher.'

117 *Le grand personnage noir*
Large black figure, 1948
Lithograph on Rives wove paper. Signed,
dated and numbered *42/50* in pencil. 562 x
412mm. Mourlot 89.
1985-5-12-11

From 1948 Miró frequently returned to
Paris to make lithographs at Mourlot's
atelier in rue de Chabrol. The collaboration
between the artist and the printer Jean
Célestin (see catalogue number 63)
produced astonishing results. As Mourlot
himself wrote:

'Whatever Miró, who hardly ever speaks,
wishes, Célestin divines; a few words
suffice to confirm that the desire of the one
has been understood by the other.'

Unlike the transfer prints of the *Barcelona
series*, this lithograph was directly worked
on the stone with a brush loaded with
tusche, a lithographic ink. The fine white
lines were scraped out of the black using a
needle. The effect produced is a subtle
balance of painterly and graphic marks.
Published in 1949, this is one of the earliest
prints to be published by Galerie Maeght
in Paris. Maeght was largely responsible
for bringing Miró's reputation as a
printmaker to a wider public after the
Second World War.

Alberto Magnelli
1888-1971

Born in Florence where he had close
contact with the Italian Futurists,
Magnelli made the first of several visits to
Paris in 1914 before settling there in 1931.
His work moved towards geometric
abstraction during the 1930s. After the
Second World War he became a leading
figure in abstract art.

118 *Untitled*, 1941
Woodcut printed in black and dark red on
a map of Grasse. Signed, dated and
inscribed: *e/a* in red ink. Verso: numbered
11 in pencil. 254 x 195mm. Maisonnier 5.
1994-6-19-5

On the arrival of the German troops in
Paris, Magnelli fled to the town of Grasse
in the South of France, where Hans Arp
and his wife Sophie Taeuber-Arp and Sonia
Delaunay, the widow of Robert Delaunay
(see catalogue number 44), were also
sheltering. Lacking conventional supports
and materials, Magnelli began to make
gouaches on writing paper and collages of
music sheets as well as four woodcuts in
1941. This woodcut is one of about ten or
twelve impressions printed on a map of
Grasse cannibalised from a contemporary
gazetteer. An ironical reference to wartime
conditions is revealed by the map's
cancellation of the Syndicat d'Initiative,
the local tourist bureau. On the verso is a
map of the region. As the name of the place
where Magnelli was staying was called
Plan-de-Grasse, the use of the map may
have been partly intended as a pun.
Stylistically the two abstract forms
overprinted onto the town plan show
Magnelli's admiration for the work of his
neighbour Arp.

Jean Fautrier
1898-1964

119 *Etude d'otages*
Study of hostages, about 1945
Photogravure, aquatint and etching on
wove paper. 2nd state. Signed and
numbered *47/50* in pencil. 303 x 284mm.
Mason 254.II.
1982-10-2-22

Shown here is one of the most haunting
evocations of the tortured victims of the
Gestapo. Fautrier has created a repeating
image in which a shaded lamp with its
restricted pool of light metamorphoses into
an expressive and fragile face. Fautrier was
arrested in January 1943 and then released.
His friend the poet Jean Paulhan found
him a safe place to work in a mental
hospital at Châtenay-Malabry outside
Paris. Horrified by the Gestapo's torture
and killing of their victims in the adjoining
woods, Fautrier began his celebrated series
of *Otages* from 1942 to 1944. This print,
made in about 1945 and published in its
first state as an illustration to Paulhan's
text *Fautrier l'enragé* (1949), is related to a
painting entitled **Le Massacre**. This
impression is from a second edition
published by Fautrier's dealer Michel
Couturier between 1960 and the artist's
death in 1964.

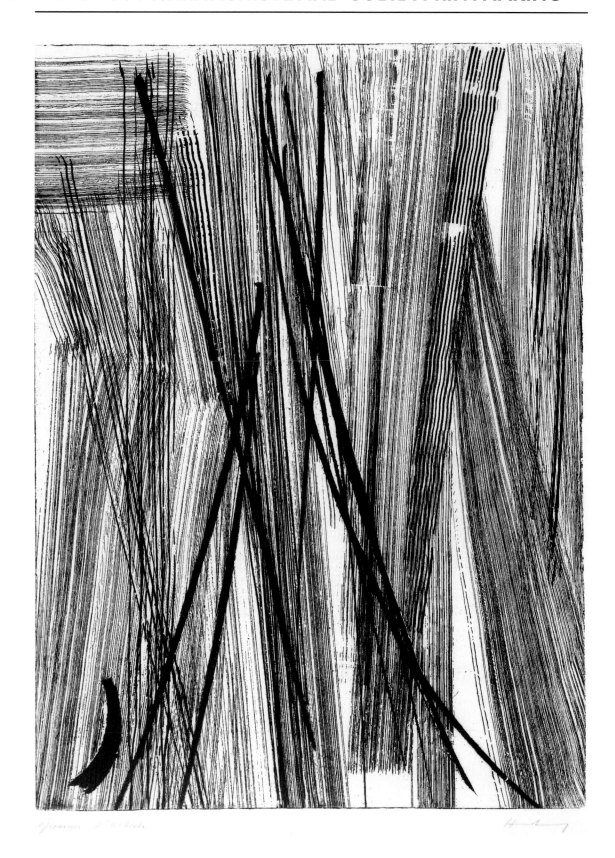

Hans Hartung
Gravure 22
1953 (catalogue number 122)
© ADGAP, Paris and DACS, London 1997

Gestural abstraction dominated avant-garde printmaking in post-war Paris. The term *Tachisme* (derived from *tacher*, to stain) was coined by French critics to describe the work of painters like Bryen, Soulages and Hartung which was characterised by expressive gestural mark-making. *Tachisme* was less concerned with the image or form but with the material presence of the work and the process of its making. To the writer Michel Tapié this was *un art autre*, 'another' art, not only different from, but indifferent to everything else that had preceded it. This aesthetic was linked to the existentialism of post-war Paris, exemplified in the philosophical writings of Jean-Paul Sartre. Initially *Tachisme* developed independently of American abstract expressionism but the arrival of the work of Pollock and de Kooning in Europe in the early 1950s gave it a powerful stimulus.

Cobra, unlike *Tachisme*, was not a term invented by critics. It was an international group of artists and poets who called themselves *CoBrA* after their cities of origin, Copenhagen, Brussels and Amsterdam, although the group was actually born in a Paris café in 1948. The Cobra artists, who included Alechinsky and Corneille (catalogue numbers 127-8) from Belgium, Jorn from Denmark and Appel from the Netherlands stood for a pluralistic, anti-hierarchic approach to art and culture, taking their inspiration from the spontaneous expression of child, folk and primitive art. Vital to their programme was printmaking, which enabled their art to reach a wider audience in keeping with their commitment to Marxism. A central figure in the group was the poet and critic Christian Dotremont who encouraged the Cobra artists to create 'word pictures' (catalogue numbers 107-8). Oriental calligraphy was a major influence on both the Cobra and Tachiste artists, whose gestural mark-making was stimulated by Zen philosophy; Alechinsky and Soulages both made separate journeys to the Far East to study calligraphy.

Although not a member of the Cobra group, which broke up in 1951, Dubuffet shared their interest in 'outsider art' (catalogue number 129). But his most important project was the remarkable *Les Phénomènes* (catalogue numbers 131-9), which investigated the phenomena of the natural world in more than 350 lithographs made between 1958 and 1962. This encyclopaedic series stands as one of the triumphs in the history of lithography.

120 *Art Abstrait*, 1946
A portfolio of twelve lithographs by
twelve artists, published by Opéra, Paris,
1946. Each print signed and numbered
26/100 in pencil.
1995-9-30-27.1-12

Jean Deyrolle 1911-1967
Opera, 1946
238 x 177mm, Richar 24,
1995-9-30-27.3

Hans Hartung 1907-1989
Untitled, 1946
230 x 175mm, Schmücking 60,
1995-9-30-27.7

Serge Poliakoff 1900-1969
Untitled, 1946
237 x 180mm, Rivière 1,
1995-9-30-27.9

Shown here are three non-objective
gestural lithographs from a portfolio of
twelve which was published under the title
Art Abstrait in Paris in 1946. The twelve
artists were Del-Marle, Dewasne, Deyrolle,
Domela, Engel-Pak, Fleischmann, Hartung,
Misztrik de Monda, Poliakoff, Marie
Raymond, Schneider and Nicolaas Warb. It
was printed by Desjobert in an edition of
100. For many of the participating artists,
including Poliakoff and Deyrolle, this
album marked their first venture in
lithography. The idea of publishing these
lithographs sprang from a series of
exhibitions devoted to abstract art which
were held in the rue Cujas of the Latin
Quarter between February and July 1946,
where, as *Art Abstrait* noted:

'... thousands of visitors, especially
students, have been able to see
representative paintings of all tendencies
of this art still so opposed, and still
unknown.'

Accompanying the portfolio was a preface
on Abstract Art by Charles Estienne, a
critic and professor of history, who was a
close friend of Deyrolle. Estienne's text
came with an English translation in which
he wrote:

'...this art work is essentially defined by
two insoluble elements ... first by a form
that excludes all literal remembrance or
citation of the naturalist exterior world;
then by an inmost necessity, making itself
its subject ... We must add to these ... this
"Aura" this particular giddiness ... gushing
out to all degrees ... the signs of life, gleams
or sparkles which each time renew the
magic gesture of creation.'

Hans Hartung
1907-1989

Born in Leipzig where he studied philosophy and art history, Hartung first came to Paris in 1926 and travelled widely before eventually settling there in 1935. Hartung was a close friend of the sculptor Julio Gonzalez (see catalogue number 111), whose daughter he married.

121 *Gravure 13*, 1953
Etching with aquatint printed in brown on heavy wove paper. Signed in pencil.
388 x 526mm. Schmücking 42.
1994-6-19-25

Hartung made his first abstract etchings in 1938, but it was in 1953 that he embarked on his impressive series of 29 gestural etchings at the Atelier Lacourière where this work was printed. The linear and painterly gestures of this print were achieved through etching and aquatint respectively. Hartung's principal publishers at this time were Berggruen in Paris and Marbach in Berne, although this print was published by Jacometti in Zurich for his *L'Oeuvre gravé* series in 1956.

122 *Gravure 22*, 1953
Etching on heavy wove paper. Signed and inscribed: *épreuve d'artiste* in pencil.
517 x 380mm. Schmücking 51.
1994-6-19-26

This was published by Berggruen in an edition of 100. Its spontaneity and directness are characteristic of Hartung's etchings of this period.

123 *Lithographie 1*, 1966
Lithograph on heavy wove paper. Signed and numbered *42/75* in pencil.
695 x 457mm.
1995-9-30-54

Hartung first took up lithography in 1946; an example (catalogue number 120) is shown in the nearby table case. In a burst of printmaking he made 80 lithographs between 1957 and 1958 which were mostly printed in Paris, either at the Atelier Pons or the Atelier Patris. Another series of 35 followed in 1963 and 1964 which were printed at St Gallen, Switzerland by the Erkerpresse. This lithograph of 1966 was printed by the same workshop in Switzerland. It shows the extraordinary way Hartung scratched out highlights from the dark lithographic wash with crayons and razors.

Pierre Soulages
born 1919

124 *Lithographie no. 6*, 1957
Lithograph printed in grey, dull blue and black on Rives wove paper. Signed and numbered *54/60* in pencil. 575 x 440mm. Rivière 6.
1995-9-30-62

This is one of seven lithographs published by Galerie Berggruen in 1957, when Soulages first took up the technique. It was printed at the Atelier Jean Pons where Hartung's lithographs of the same year were also printed. As in his gestural paintings of this period, Soulages' marks on the stone are extremely controlled. The simplicity and grandeur of his work derives in part from the artist's fascination with the Romanesque churches in the Aveyron region of the Massif Central where he was brought up. Soulages' use of dark and sombre colours is also related to his interest in oriental calligraphy and its associations with poetry and painting.

Camille Bryen
1907-1977

Born in Nantes, Bryen came to Paris in 1926 where he soon moved in Surrealist circles, forming close artistic friendships with Ubac (catalogue number 103) and the poet Tristan Tzara during the 1930s. Although he exhibited his first 'tachiste' work in 1936, it was only after 1945 that his style fully developed. His earliest prints were drypoints made in 1948. In all he made some 90 etchings and 23 lithographs. The impetus for much of Bryen's printmaking came from his association with the existentialist poets and writers, including René Crevel and Antonin Artaud.

125 *Cerf-Volant*
Kite, 1960
Lithograph printed in five colours on Rives wove paper. Signed and inscribed: *épr. d'artiste* in pencil. 600 x 480mm.
Loyer 44.
1995-9-30-53

Printed in Paris by the Atelier Patris in an edition of 100, this is one of five colour lithographs and six colour etchings of Bryen published by Nesto Jacometti in Zurich between 1951 and 1967. *Cerf-Volant* was included in Jacometti's *L'Oeuvre gravé* series which was widely distributed through Europe during this period. This publishing enterprise greatly facilitated the spread of Tachiste ideas outside France.

126 *Ensemble éclaté*
Burst ensemble, 1964
Etching and aquatint printed in red,
green and black on Arches wove paper.
Signed and numbered *33/80* in pencil.
340 x 279mm. Loyer 60.
1995-7-23-2

This was printed from three plates, one for
each colour, by Georges Visat in Paris. In
all Visat printed 23 of Bryen's etchings and
drypoints between 1950 and 1968. Bryen
provided a statement of his existentialist
aesthetic for Michel Seuphor's *A
Dictionary of Abstract Painting* (1958), first
published in French in 1957:

'Painting is the expression of the inner life,
and its nature is that of a cosmic function.
Far from being a simple product of sensory
excitation, it should, in its proper capacity,
act like a magical phenomenon making
itself felt not only through the optical, but
through the para-optical perception, not
only through the dimensions of shapes and
colours present, but also through what is
not present, through memory and the
ambivalences of the physical and psychical
personality.'

Corneille
born 1922
Belgian born of Dutch parents, Corneille
was a leading figure of the Cobra group
and worked in Paris from 1950.

127 *L'Oiseleur*
The birdcatcher, 1953
Colour aquatint and soft-ground etching
on wove paper watermarked Johannot.
Signed, dated, titled and numbered *2/20*
in pencil. 149 x 108mm. Donkersloot-Van
den Berghe 26.
1994-5-15-39

Corneille has used gauze pressed into the
softground to create the cloud forms
against which the stylised birdcatcher is
silhouetted. This etching was printed at
Hayter's Atelier 17 in Paris. Printed in 1953
with a turquoise background tone, this
comes from the first edition of twenty
impressions. A second edition of 25, on a
yellow background, was published in
Amsterdam in 1989.

128 *Le Masque*
The mask, 1953
Lithograph printed in beige and black on
Arches wove paper. Signed, titled,
numbered *7/12* and dated: *15-4-53* in
pencil. 290 x 369mm. Donkersloot-Van
den Berghe 29.
1993-6-20-36

Also titled *The first awakening in the
desert*, this is one of six lithographs
printed by Dorphinand in Paris for
Corneille in 1953. While the figures in this
print share a certain affinity with those in
Dubuffet's lithographs of this date, they
seem to dematerialize into the landscape.
They recall the way sand, wind and sun
obliterate all the physical features in the
Saharan desert, from which Corneille had
returned two years earlier.

Jean Dubuffet
1901-1985

After a mixed start working in his family's wine business, Dubuffet finally embarked on his career in 1942, when, through the poet Jean Paulhan, he was introduced to Fautrier (catalogue number 119) and the writers Seghers, Eluard (see catalogue number 109), Guillevic and Ponge. From 1947 Dubuffet began to exhibit and write about 'outsider art', the work of naive artists and the mentally disturbed, which he had been collecting since the 1920s. Convinced that as much good art was made outside the artistic professions as within, Dubuffet determined to broaden art by founding the *Société de l'Art Brut*. The figurative imagery of catalogue numbers 129 and 130 are informed by Dubuffet's passion for what he called *art brut* (raw art).

129   *Nutrition*, 1944
> Lithograph. Signed in pencil. 290 x 170mm. Webel 22.
> On loan from the Hunterian Art Gallery, University of Glasgow. Acc. no. 21174

This comes from Dubuffet's first illustrated book *Matière et mémoire, ou les lithographes à l'école* published in an edition of 60 by Mourlot in 1945. The text is a treatise on lithography written by the poet Francis Ponge whose poetic explanation takes its title from the influential text of the philosopher Henri Bergson. The 34 lithographs accompanying the publication were produced at the Atelier Mourlot from September 1944. Made under Mourlot's expert tutelage, these prints were a considerable advance on Dubuffet's first essays in the technique which his neighbour, the printer Jean Pons, had introduced to him a few months earlier. Over the next 30 years Dubuffet was to become one of the most prolific printmakers working in Paris, making nearly 1,500 prints.

130   *Chat furieux*
Angry cat, 1953
> Lithograph on Arches wove paper. Signed, dated, titled and inscribed: *épreuve d'essai* with dedication: *affecteusement à Edith* in pencil. 277 x 407mm. Webel 359.
> 1991-10-5-76

Shown here is one of Dubuffet's *Assemblages d'empreintes* (Imprint assemblages), a group of 27 lithographs he made in 1953. The series grew out of the idea of cutting and reassembling pieces of paper mottled with indian ink. The accidental forms created were often suggestive of recognisable images. Speaking of the lithographs, Dubuffet wrote:

'... they resulted from imprints made with greasy ink on sheets of transfer paper. I cut pieces out of these sheets, stuck them together with paste and finally transferred the whole thing to the stone.'

Les Phénomènes, 1958-62

After an absence of five years, Dubuffet returned to printmaking in 1958 when he embarked on his long series *Phénomènes*, an encyclopaedic project which would result in 362 lithographs issued in 24 albums, from 1958 to 1962. In order to produce this ambitious series Dubuffet set up his own lithographic workshop in the rue de Rennes, working closely with the master printer Serge Lozingot. As well as referring to the soil, which he had recently explored in his paintings, Dubuffet wanted to expand the repertoire to include 'all sorts of other elements or phenomena' of the natural world 'such as water, wind, sky, foliations or germinations, to the point of looking very much like an attempt to establish a repertory of all possible facts one can see or even think.' The British Museum has a complete set of *Banalités*; this comprises 10 plates of the sixth album in colour published in 1961. It also has individual plates from several of the other albums in *Les Phénomènes*. All come from the collection of Mr and Mrs Ralph F. Colin, close friends of Dubuffet and his most important American collectors.

131 **Les Fruits de la terre**
The Fruits of the Earth, 1959
Plate 14 from *Théâtre du sol*, 8th album. Lithograph on Rives wove paper. Signed, dated, titled and inscribed: *épreuve d'essai* in pencil. 545 x 400mm. Webel 540.
1995-9-30-16

132 **Le vent et l'eau**
Wind and water, 1959
Plate 3 from *Eaux, pierres, sable*, 10th album. Lithograph on heavy japanese paper. Signed, dated, titled and inscribed: *épreuve d'artiste* in pencil. 531 x 389mm. Webel 565.
1995-9-30-18

133 **Géométrie**, 1959
Plate 16 from *Sites et chaussées*, 12th album. Lithograph on Arches wove paper. Signed, dated, titled and inscribed: *épreuve d'artiste* in pencil. 531 x 391mm. Webel 614.
1995-9-30-22

134 **Allégresse**
Joy, 1959
Plate 5 from *L'Arpenteur*, 3rd album in colour. Lithograph in eight colours on Arches wove paper. Signed, dated, titled and inscribed: *épreuve d'artiste* in pencil. 475 x 349mm. Webel 659.
1995-9-30-25

135 **Esplanade ombreuse**
Shady esplanade, 1958
Plate 2 from *Banalités*, 6th album in colour. Lithograph in four colours on Arches wove paper. Signed, dated, titled and inscribed: *épreuve d'artiste* in pencil. 300 x 395mm. Webel 686.
1995-9-30-3

136 **Voie lactée noire**
Black Milky Way, 1958
Plate 4 from *Banalités*, 6th album in colour. Lithograph in five colours on Arches wove paper. Signed, dated, titled and inscribed: *épreuve d'artiste* in pencil. 381 x 305mm. Webel 688.
1995-9-30-5

137 **Rideau d'interdit**
Curtain of the forbidden, 1958
Plate 7 from *Banalités*, 6th album in colour. Lithograph in three colours on Arches wove paper. Signed, dated, titled and inscribed: *épreuve d'artiste* in pencil. 400 x 320mm. Webel 691.
1995-9-30-8

138 **Sombre développement**, 1959
Plate 8 from *Banalités*, 6th album in colour. Lithograph in three colours on Arches wove paper. Signed, dated, titled and inscribed: *épreuve d'artiste* in pencil. 511 x 391mm. Webel 692.
1995-9-30-9

139 **Mûrissement**
Ripening, 1959
Plate 10 from *Banalités*, 6th album in colour. Lithograph in five colours on Arches wove paper. Signed, dated, titled and inscribed: *épreuve d'artiste* in pencil. 475 x 369mm. Webel 694.
1995-9-30-11

Pierre Courtin
born 1921

140 *Untitled*, 1946
Engraving on a piece of Swiss newspaper. Signed, dated and numbered *2/4* in pencil. 118 x 90mm. Rivière 22.
1996-6-8-8

There are only four impressions of this print; all of them printed on the unconventional support of a piece of newspaper. Used here is a piece from the Swiss bilingual paper *Neue Zürcher Zeitung*. It was applied to a sheet of white laid paper in a manner similar to chine collé. Courtin was greatly interested in trying out different types of paper on which to make his prints. This print belongs to a handful of engravings in which Courtin was experimenting with a style close to that of Bryen.

141 *17 Février 1949*
Engraving on textured paper. Signed, titled with the date: *17 février 1949* and numbered *5/30* in pencil. 345 x 263mm. Rivière 61.
1996-6-8-9

Courtin began to make constructivist engravings in 1945; this style largely dominated his work for the next five years. In 1944, Courtin had met Domela, Poliakoff and the other abstract painters around the critic Charles Estienne (see catalogue number 120), whose work had a strong influence on him. From 1947 until 1951, Courtin was employed as a printer in the intaglio workshop of Leblanc, where he forged a close professional friendship with Villon whose late etchings he helped to print.

142 *Prégiottesque*, 5 October 1964
Engraving printed in relief on a thick hand-made paper. Signed, titled, dated: *5 octobre 1964* and numbered *1/4* in pencil. 389 x 334mm. Rivière 350.
1995-2-26-3

Courtin began making engravings printed in relief from 1950. Hayter described Courtin's method as a development of experiments made by Negri (catalogue number 105), Brignoni and himself in the 1930s, in which the plate was hollowed out to print in white relief. In his revised edition of *New Ways of Gravure* (New York: Watson Guptill Publications, 1981, p. 103), Hayter wrote:

'Courtin carves into the soft metal to make a matrix from which, with slight general inking, a relief of sculptural, even monumental, character is formed under the press. The print thus becomes a relief in itself, the cast from the hollowed-out plate having the character of carved metal rather than the pictural quality of most printmaking.'

Because Courtin worked on zinc which was a softer metal than copper, not more than five engravings could generally be pulled; in this case only four impressions were made. Courtin habitually used yellow or clear inks on the plate; often, as in this print, they slightly oxidised from contact with the zinc. The paper that Courtin used for these relief prints is particularly thick, often being made up of several thicknesses laminated together. This enabled him to get a much greater relief.

Serge Poliakoff
Composition brune, ocre, blanche et rouge
Composition brown, ochre, white and red
1953 (catalogue number 151)

Artists had been starved of materials during the Second World War (see catalogue number 118) and there had been relatively little colour printmaking during the inter-war years. This was to change from the late 1940s with the availability in Paris of well-equipped lithographic workshops staffed by highly skilled printers such as Mourlot and Pons. These facilities attracted both publishers and artists.

In 1949 the publisher Pierre Cailler initiated his colour print series *Guilde de la gravure* from Geneva, although the lithographs were nearly all printed in Paris. The modest price and decorative colour of these uniformly sized prints by artists like Manessier and Poliakoff contributed to their success. In 1954, Nesto Jacometti, Cailler's artistic director, set up his own publishing concern *L'Oeuvre Gravé* in Zurich in imitation of Cailler. These two print publishers, who between them published nearly 1500 prints up to 1971, greatly contributed to the dissemination of School of Paris printmaking.

Compared with developments in America, artists in France were relatively late in taking up the screenprint, although it appears this technique was already known to Vasarely and Domela by the 1930s. *Pochoir*, the French term for stencil, had been much used by School of Paris artists as a reproductive technique for making colour prints, such as fashion plates and book illustrations, since before the First World War. In the early 1950s pochoir and the related technique of screenprinting was taken up by the hard-edge abstractionists, such as Vasarely, Deyrolle and Dewasne, for the translation of their paintings into prints. The screenprint, rather than colour lithography, was the ideal technique for achieving their hard-edged shapes and intense matt colours. Working in collaboration with these artists was the Cuban printer Arcay who was responsible for the reproductive screenprints issued in portfolios by the publisher André Bloc and the gallery Denise René.

Alfred Manessier
1911-1993

143 *Crépuscule*
Dusk, 1950
Four-colour lithograph in crimson,
yellow ochre, turquoise and black. Signed
and numbered *17/200* in pencil.
404 x 263mm.
1995-9-30-58

144 *Crépuscule*
Dusk, 1950
Four-colour lithograph in dark yellow
ochre, turquoise, crimson and black.
Signed and inscribed in pencil: *Epreuve
d'artiste 6/ Série anglaise*. 404 x 263mm.
1995-9-30-57

This print was published in Geneva by
Pierre Cailler in 1950 in the first series of
the *Guilde de la Gravure*; it was issued as
no. 59 out of 455 in the series, which
continued until 1967. The price in 1950 was
15 Swiss francs. Catalogue number 144 is
an artist's proof printed from the same
stones as those of the main edition but in a
different colour sequence; it is inscribed
série anglaise. It may have been part of a
group of impressions sent to London,
possibly to the Redfern Gallery, which
distributed many of the School of Paris
colour prints to the English market
throughout the 1950s and 1960s. The shapes
in Manessier's ostensibly abstract works of
this period derive from the changing
patterns of the coast and harbour at the
mouth of the Somme, the landscape of his
youth, which he regularly revisited
between 1948 and 1955.

145 *Gethsemani*, 1951
Five-colour lithograph in blue, green,
purple, red and black. Signed and
numbered *50/200* in pencil. 339 x 520mm.
1995-9-30-56

The subject of this print could be read as
the tomb of Christ. Manessier was
profoundly influenced by the ascetic and
penitential life of the Trappist monks,
which he had first experienced on a retreat
at the Trappist monastery of Soligny in
1943. Much of his art, particularly in the
field of stained glass windows (of which he
designed nearly 250), was devoted to the
expression of his deep Catholic faith.
Printed in an edition of 200, this was
published in Geneva as no. 118 in the series
Guilde de la Gravure; the drystamp of
Cailler's series is visible lower left.

Jean Dewasne
born 1921

146 *Untitled*, 1953
> Five-colour stencil on wove paper. Signed and numbered *53/100* in pencil.
> 237 x 315mm.
> 1995-9-30-63

This and catalogue numbers 147-9 come from an album of five plates by five artists entitled *Dewasne - Deyrolle - Jacobsen - Mortensen - Vasarely*. Published by Editions Denise René in an edition of 100, the album coincided with a group exhibition of their recent work at the Galerie Denise René in January 1953. The prints were all produced as colour stencils, or pochoirs, at the Ateliers Renson in Paris. Characteristic of the hard-edge abstract prints in this album is the intense, flat colour achieved by brushing gouache pigments through the open areas of the stencil onto the paper below. Dewasne began to show his hard-edge geometrical paintings at Galerie Denise René from 1946. With Pillet he founded in 1950 the Atelier d'Art Abstrait in Montparnasse where Dewasne's course on the technology of painting involved the study of the chemistry of colours, theories of vision and problems of plastic technique. Friends with Hartung, Poliakoff and Deyrolle, in 1952 he wrote a book on Vasarely.

Jean Deyrolle
1911-1967

A close friend of Magnelli (catalogue number 118), Deyrolle freed himself from figuration in 1944. His abstract paintings were regularly shown at the Galerie Denise René from 1946. While his first lithograph was printed in Paris for *Art Abstrait* (catalogue number 120), from 1949 Deyrolle made periodic visits to Copenhagen where he produced several albums of lithographs which were jointly published by the Danish printer Sorensen and Denise René in Paris.

147 *Denise*, 1953
> Five-colour stencil on wove paper. Signed and numbered *53/100* in pencil. 227 x 297mm. Richar 80.
> 1995-9-30-64

Printed in three shades of grey, red and black, this was titled after the publisher Denise René. Deyrolle made three other pochoirs in 1952 at the Ateliers Renson, all named after close friends such as the painter Edgar Pillet and the dealer Colette Allendy.

Richard Mortensen
1910-1993

Born in Copenhagen, Mortensen was a co-founder, in 1934, of the Danish painting group and associated periodical *Linien* (The Line), which brought the developments of the Paris avant-garde to a Danish audience during the 1930s. After the war Mortensen lived with his compatriot, the sculptor Robert Jacobsen, in Paris where his work was exhibited at the Galerie Denise René from 1948. During the 1950s he made many screenprints after his gouaches. Most of these were printed by Wifredo Arcay and published by Denise René, including the album *Mortensen-Vasarely* which coincided with their joint exhibition in December 1956. In all Mortensen made over 500 prints.

148 *Untitled*, 1953
> Nine-colour stencil on wove paper.
> Signed and numbered *53/100* in pencil.
> 272 x 201mm. Frandsen 15.
> 1995-9-30-66

This is after Mortensen's painting entitled **Composition sur fond gris** of 1950. Two months after Denise René issued this pochoir in her album of January 1953, Mortensen used the same painting for a lithograph which was published jointly by Christian Sorensen in Copenhagen and Denise René in Paris.

Victor Vasarely
1908-1997

Born in Hungary where he trained at the 'Muhely', a Bauhaus-inspired academy in Budapest, Vasarely settled in Paris in 1930. In 1940 he met Denise René whom he persuaded to open a gallery in rue la Boëtie. The inaugural exhibition in November 1944 was devoted to Vasarely's 'graphic studies'. These were connected to his researches into optical effects and black-and-white experiments with stripes, checkerboard and zebra patterns. In 1955 Vasarely organised an exhibition of kinetic objects at the Galerie Denise René and published his *Manifeste jaune*, which marked the birth of kinetic art. The Galerie Denise René continued to publish a prodigious number of Vasarely's screenprints during the 1950s and 1960s; these were invariably printed by the Cuban artist and printmaker Wifredo Arcay working closely with the artist.

149 *Untitled*, 1953
> Colour stencil on wove paper. Signed and numbered *53/100* in pencil. 267 x 200mm. Stedelijk 3.
> 1995-9-30-67

This is from Denise René's album of five pochoir plates published in January 1953. The colours and the composition of this print recall those in the contemporary work of Herbin and Magnelli. The vase-like shape has a distant echo of the Purist works of Léger and Le Corbusier of the late 1920s.

Jean Deyrolle
1911-1967

150 *La Cité modèle*
The model city, 1954
Seven-colour screenprint on wove paper.
Signed in pencil; inscribed: *e/a 1/5* in blue
ink. 541 x 334mm. Richar 95.
1995-9-30-68

This was Deyrolle's only screenprint. Like
catalogue number 151, it comes from the
portfolio *Jeune Peintres d'Aujourd'hui*
published by André Bloc in 1954. This
contained sixteen screenprints by sixteen
artists, most of whom were hard-edge
abstractionists. These included the
sculptor-publisher Bloc, Dewasne,
Jacobsen, Leppien, Mortensen, Pillet,
Poliakoff and Vasarely. Printed in an
edition of 300 by Arcay, the portfolio was
published with an accompanying preface
by Léon Degand. In October 1954 it was
exhibited at the Galérie Denise René in the
exhibition *Sérigraphies*. Deyrolle's
composition is related to the huge picture
he painted for the exhibition *La Cité
modèle* at the Musée d'Art Moderne de la
Ville de Paris in 1954.

Serge Poliakoff
1900-1969
Born in Moscow with aristocratic
connections, Poliakoff was forced to flee by
the Russian Revolution in 1919 and settled
in Paris in 1923. Kandinsky was among the
earliest admirers of his abstract paintings,
which he began to show from 1938. His
mature abstract pictures date from 1945.
He was closely involved in the exhibitions
organised by the Centre des Recherches at
rue Cujas in 1946, when his first lithograph
was published in the album *Art Abstrait*
(catalogue number 120). Poliakoff only
made five screenprints.

151 *Composition brune, ocre,
blanche et rouge*
**Composition brown, ochre,
white and red**, 1953
Four-colour screenprint on heavy wove
paper. Signed and dated: *IX 53* on the
screen. 445 x 330mm. Rivière 4.
1995-9-30-59

His first screenprint, this comes from
Jeune Peintres d'Aujourd'hui (see
catalogue number 150), the second
portfolio of screenprints published by
André Bloc's Editions Art d'Aujourd'hui in
1954. In 1953, Bloc had published his first
portfolio, *Maîtres d'Aujourd'hui*, which
also contained sixteen screenprints, all
reproductions after paintings.

152 *Composition brune, jaune et rouge*
Composition brown, yellow and red, 1954
Three-colour lithograph on wove paper.
Signed and inscribed: *E.A* in pencil. 312 x
215mm. Rivière 5.
1995-9-30-60

Printed by the Atelier Jean Pons, this lithograph was published by the Galerie Bing in a large unnumbered edition to coincide with Poliakoff's one-man show at the gallery in October 1954. It was also used for the exhibition poster and invitation cards. Pons printed most of Poliakoff's lithographs from 1953 to 1964, 33 in all. Poliakoff's prints were all based on earlier gouaches that he had judged particularly suitable for interpretation, but he always worked in close collaboration with his printer. He heightened some of his proofs with gouache, where he was attempting to recapture the intensity of the light in his originals. Poliakoff made some 80 lithographs in all, several of which were published posthumously. Many of his lithographs were produced for publishers outside France, such as Nesto Jacometti's *L'Oeuvre Gravé* in Zurich, *La Guilde de la Lithographie* in Ostende and, in particular, for Im Erker in St Gallen, Switzerland.

Pablo Picasso
Deux femmes au réveil
Two women waking up
1959 (printed 1964) (catalogue number 159)
© Succession Picasso/DACS 1997

From the 1950s until his death in 1973, Picasso produced an astonishing number of prints which showed no diminution of his creative powers and technical invention. In 1959 he took up the linocut and for the next four years experimented with its possibilities in the most original way. Whereas traditionally a new block was cut for each colour, Picasso developed the 'reductive method' whereby a single block was cut and printed across the entire edition before further cutting and printing of the same block with the next colour. Although this meant that no changes could be made once the sequence had begun, Picasso could forsee the cumulative build up of colour and design. His printer Hidalgo Arnéra once said that Picasso 'had a sort of aggressive delight in encountering an obstacle and surmounting and conquering it' (cited in Pat Gilmour, 'Picasso and his Printers', *The Print Collector's Newsletter*, vol. 18, no. 3 (July-August 1987), p. 88). His final innovation with lino was the 'rinsed' linocut (see catalogue number 159) which created an effect rather like a ghostly negative.

In 1961 Picasso married Jacqueline Roque and moved to his new villa Notre-Dame-de-Vie in Mougins where he lived until his death. From 1963 he returned to making etchings with the brothers Aldo and Piero Crommelynck whom he had known in Paris since the early 1950s and who had now set up a workshop for proofing plates close to him in Mougins. In 1968, when Picasso was in his late 80s, he produced with Atelier Crommelynck no less than 347 etchings in just six months; these show an extraordinary technical diversity and inventiveness and count among his greatest prints (catalogue number 162). In 1970, he began the 156 series of erotic etchings (catalogue number 163); the last print was made a year before Picasso's death, on 8 April 1973.

Pablo Picasso
1881-1973

153 *Le Picador*, 1952
Aquatint on heavy Arches wove paper. Dated on the plate: *18 juin 52*. Signed and inscribed: *Bon à tirer* in pencil. 458 x 553mm. Bloch 692; Baer 894.Ba.
1994-10-2-8

The Spanish bullfight, earlier explored in the mid-1930s (see catalogue numbers 60-1), became an increasingly significant theme in Picasso's prints of the 1950s, where it was expressed with great technical virtuosity in aquatint, lithography and linocut. Shown here is an aquatint of 1952 freely and boldly brushed onto the plate. The spectator's head above the barrier recalls motifs in the work of Goya, Picasso's great predecessor, whose experiments with aquatint were the first masterpieces in the technique. This proof is inscribed *Bon à tirer* by Picasso, thereby giving his approval to the printer Roger Lacourière to begin printing the edition of 50. It was published in 1952 by Galerie Louise Leiris which became the principal publisher of Picasso's prints in the 1960s.

154 *La Pique III*
The pike III, 1959
Lithograph on Arches wove paper. Dated on the zinc plate: *2.9.59*. Undescribed 1st state. 502 x 658mm. Mourlot 326.
1994-10-2-9.1
Presented by Dr Frederick Mulder

155 *La Pique III*
The pike III, 1959
Lithograph on Arches wove paper. Dated on the zinc plate: *2.9.59*. Undescribed 3rd state. 502 x 658mm. Mourlot 326.
1994-10-2-9.2.

According to Mourlot only three proofs of this print were pulled before the zinc plate was abandoned. Shown here is a proof of the first state (catalogue number 154) worked principally in crayon and another of the third state (catalogue number 155) after the zinc plate had been flooded with lithographic wash. An attempt was made to recover the design by drawing outlines with a needle, such as for the horns of the bull. But, as Mourlot, noted:

'... this plate did not stand up to the printing of proofs and became clogged after the first proofs; owing to this bad result, it was polished out.'

Curiously enough, a proof of the second state turned up at Christie's, London (27 June 1996, lot 636).

156 *Pique II*
Pike II, 1959
Colour linocut on Arches wove paper. 530 x 640mm. Bloch 911; Baer 1228.Bb1.
1994-10-2-10

This was made between 31 August and 31 October 1959 at Cannes where Picasso had bought the villa La Californie in 1955. From 1959, over the next four years, Picasso would exhaust the technical possibilities of making colour prints from linoleum. This was printed in four colours, light caramel, terracotta, dark brown and black, from two blocks.

157 *Portrait de Jacqueline accoudée, au collier*
Portrait of Jacqueline with necklace, resting on her elbow, 1959
Colour linocut on Arches wove paper. Dated on the block: *24. 11.59.* 635 x 528mm. Bloch 928; Baer 1258.IIA. 1994-10-2-11

Made in Cannes on 24 November 1959, this linocut was cut by the reductive method from one block and printed in three colours light caramel, dark brown and black. The subject is Jacqueline Roque, whom Picasso had met in 1953 after the departure of Françoise Gilot with her two children, Claude and Paloma. Jacqueline, whom he later married in 1961, appears in many of his linocuts. In this highly complex image, Picasso shows her both in profile and full face but within the design conceals a portrait of himself kissing her lips. This is a proof outside the edition of 50 published by Galerie Louise Leiris in 1960.

158 *Deux femmes au réveil*
Two women waking up, 1959
Colour linocut on Arches wove paper. Inscribed in pencil: *Femme regardant par la fenêtre* and *1959 - 3 couleurs*. Printer's stamp in blue ink: *Imprimerie Arnera/ Epreuve d' Atelier/ Hors Commerce.* Another on verso. 533 x 640mm. Bloch 925; Baer 1249.IIBb. 1996-4-27-1

The subject recalls Picasso's earlier treatment of this theme in the lithographs of 1945 (see catalogue numbers 63-4). In this linocut made in Cannes on 8 November 1959, a young woman rises from her bed to draw open the curtain; her companion, still drowsy with sleep, shields herself from the sudden burst of light. The morning sunlight is brilliantly evoked by the use of a warm caramel colour. It was printed by Arnéra using the same three colours as catalogue number 157.

159 *Deux femmes au réveil*
Two women waking up, 1959
(printed 1964)
'Rinsed' linocut printed in white ink and brushed over with indian ink wash and rinsed, on Arches wove paper. Signed in red crayon. Verso: dated with ink and brush: *3.1.64.* 619 x 749mm. Baer 1249.IIC. 1996-4-27-2

Picasso's final experiment with linoleum was the 'rinsed' linocut. The work shown here was printed by Arnéra in white greasy ink from the remains of the block used for *Deux femmes au réveil* (catalogue number 158). The still wet impression would be hurried round to Picasso's studio where he and Jacqueline would don bathroom robes and proceed to 'rinse' the proof in the bath with indian ink and brush. The indian ink would be absorbed by the areas of unprinted paper and repelled by the greasy white ink in the printed areas. One witness to this 'bathtub ceremony', as Picasso called it, reported:

'Picasso is able to treat each impression as a different work, bringing out or toning down the lines by layering on the ink heavily or lightly.' (Siegfried and Angela Rosengart, *Calling on Picasso*, Lucerne, n.p., cited in Gilmour 1987, p. 88)

One of five 'rinsed' impressions of this subject, this example is dated by Picasso on the verso *3.1.64*. The two linocuts reveal how differently Picasso could work, even from the same printing matrix. Here, in a work which hovers between drawing and printmaking, Picasso transforms the earlier morning scene into a spectral nightmare, full of anxiety and foreboding.

160 **_Peintre au travail_**
   Painter at work, 1963
   Soft-ground etching printed in bistre on
   japanese tissue. Dated on the plate:
   1.11.63. 318 x 417mm. Bloch 1121;
   Baer 1115.B.
   1995-12-10-3
   Presented anonymously

In 1963 Picasso returned to etching, which
was to dominate his printmaking almost
entirely until his death ten years later. This
shows the painter in the studio, a recurrent
theme of Picasso's work. Here a female
nude observes the artist painting a seated
male model. Made at Mougins, on 1
November 1963, the plate was printed by
Atelier Crommelynck for the publisher
Louise Leiris in an edition of 50 four years
later. This example, printed very lightly in
a bistre colour, is probably a trial proof.

161 **_Dans l'atelier_**
   In the studio, 1963
   Aquatint and etching on Rives wove
   paper. Dated on the plate: *8.11.63*. Signed
   and numbered *29/50* in pencil. 314 x
   415mm. Bloch 1123; Baer 1117.IIIBb.
   1993-7-25-1

Made at Mougins on 8 November 1963, a
week later than catalogue number 160, this
shows the painter working on a portrait of
a young man whose profile can be seen at
the extreme left. The scene is observed by a
female nude seated on a dais in a pose
reminiscent of an enthroned deity. The
artist himself is depicted like a tribal fetish
and recalls the early interest Picasso took
in African art at the beginning of his
career. Like catalogue number 160, this
etching was printed by Atelier
Crommelynck and published by Galerie
Louise Leiris in 1967.

162 **_Aquatinte 26 mai 1968 III_**, 1968
   Sugar aquatint on Rives wove paper.
   Dated on the plate: *26.5.68 III*. Signed
   and numbered *18/50* in pencil. 235 x
   330mm. Bloch 1594; Baer 1610.Bbl.
   1993-10-3-1

This plate is no. 114 from the series known
as '347' and was the third of four plates
which Picasso completed on the same day,
26 May 1968. It shows a young Spanish
courtier bowing before a naked courtesan
under the watchful eye of an evil-looking
elderly duenna. The subject was inspired
by *La Célestine*, the picaresque novel of
Fernando de Rojas, first published in 1501,
for an edition of which Picasso also made
66 etched illustrations. In this example he
experimented with sugar aquatint on a
greased plate to create a mottled effect,
particularly noticeable on the costumes.
The plate was printed by Atelier
Crommelynck in an edition of 50 for
Galerie Louise Leiris in 1969.

163 **_4 avril 1971_**, 1971
   Etching on Rives wove paper. Dated on
   the plate: *Dimanche 4 avril 71*. Signed
   with stamped signature and numbered
   40/50 in pencil. 366 x 492mm. Bloch 1964;
   Baer 1973.Ba.
   1993-10-3-2

Célestine, the procuress duenna of
catalogue number 162, reappears here in
this etching of 1971. The girls preening and
chattering in the brothel are 'observed' by
a framed portrait of Degas hanging on the
right-hand wall. A great admirer of Degas,
Picasso owned at least two of his
monotypes of brothel interiors, made
around 1879. Made on Sunday 4 April 1971,
this plate is no. 109 from the erotic series
known as '156', which Picasso made at the
end of his life.

LIST OF BOOKS REFERRED TO IN ABBREVIATED FORM

Adhémar
Jean Adhémar, *Derain*, exhibition catalogue, Paris, Bibliothèque Nationale, 1955

Baer
Brigitte Baer, *Picasso Peintre-Graveur*, 7 vols and addendum vol., Berne: Editions Kornfeld, 1986-96

Black and Moorhead
Peter Black and Désirée Moorhead, *The Prints of Stanley William Hayter: A complete catalogue*, London: Phaidon Press, 1992

Bloch
Georges Bloch, *Pablo Picasso. Catalogue de l'oeuvre gravé et lithographié*, 3 vols, Berne: Editions Kornfeld et Klipstein, vol. I (1904-1967), vol. II (1966-1969), vol. IV (1970-1972), 1974-79

Bouvet
Francis Bouvet, *Bonnard: The complete graphic work*, London: Thames and Hudson, 1981

Chapon and Rouault
François Chapon and Isabelle Rouault, *Rouault, oeuvre gravé*, 2 vols, Monte-Carlo, Monaco: Editions André Sauret, 1978

Donkersloot-Van den Berghe
Patricia Donkersloot-Van den Berghe and Graham Birtwistle, *Corneille: The complete graphic works, 1948-1975*, Amsterdam: Meulenhoff, 1992

Dufresne
Thomas Dufresne, 'Charles Dufresne: L'oeuvre gravé catalogue complet', *Nouvelles de L'Estampe*, no. 134 (May 1994), pp. 3-39

Dupin
Jacques Dupin, *Miró Engraver, I. 1928-1960*, Paris: Daniel Lelong, 1984

Duthuit
Marguerite Duthuit-Matisse and Claude Duthuit with the collaboration of Françoise Garnaud, *Henri Matisse. Catalogue raisonné de l'oeuvre gravé*, 2 vols, Paris, 1983

Frandsen
Jan Würtz Frandsen, *Richard Mortensen: L'Oeuvre graphique 1942-1993*, Copenhagen: Borgens Forlag and Statens Museum for Kunst, 1995

Ginestet and Pouillon
Colette de Ginestet and Catherine Pouillon, *Jacques Villon: Les estampes et les illustrations*, Paris: Arts et Métiers Graphiques, 1979

Hacker
P.M.S. Hacker (editor), *Gravure and grace: The engravings of Roger Vieillard*, Oxford: Ashmolean Museum in association with Scolar Press, 1993

Hemin, Krohg, Perls, Rambert
Yves Hemin, Guy Krohg, Klaus Perls and Abel Rambert, *Pascin: Catalogue raisonné*, Simplicissimus, *gravures, lithographies, illustrations, sculptures, objets*, Paris: Editions Abel Rambert, 1990

Laboureur
Sylvain Laboureur, *Catalogue complet de l'oeuvre de Jean-Emile Laboureur, Tome I: Gravures etlithographies individuelles*, Neuchâtel: Ides et Calendes, 1989

Loyer
Jacqueline Loyer, 'L'Oeuvre gravé et lithographié de Bryen', *Nouvelles de l'Estampe*, no. 22 (July-August 1975), pp. 8-27, 59

Loyer
Jacqueline Loyer, 'L'Oeuvre gravé de Albert Gleizes', *Nouvelles de L'Estampe*, no. 26 (March-April 1976), pp. 11-22

Loyer and Perussaux
Jacqueline Loyer and Charles Perussaux, 'Robert Delaunay: Catalogue de son oeuvre lithographique', *Nouvelles de L'Estampe*, no. 15 (May-June 1974), pp. 3-9

Maisonnier
Anne Maisonnier, *Magnelli, l'oeuvre gravé*, Paris: Bibliothèque Nationale, 1980

Marchesseau
Daniel Marchesseau, *Marie Laurencin: Catalogue raisonné de l'oeuvre gravé*, Tokyo: Kyuryudo, 1977

Mason
Rainer Michael Mason, *Jean Fautrier: Les estampes*, Geneva, Cabinet des Estampes, 1986

Meloni
Francesco Meloni, *Gino Severini, tutta l'opera grafica*, Reggio Emilia: Libreria Prandi, 1992

Milet
Solange Milet, *Louis Marcoussis: Catalogue raisonné de l'oeuvre gravé*, Copenhagen: Forlaget Cordelia, 1991

Mourlot
Fernand Mourlot, *Picasso Lithographs*, Paris: André Sauret-Les Editions du Livre, 1970

Mourlot
Fernand Mourlot, *Joan Miró Lithographs*, vol. 1, New York: Tudor Publishing Company, 1972

Richar
Georges Richar, *Deyrolle, l'oeuvre gravé*, Paris: A.A.J.D., 1976

Rivière
Yves Rivière, *Pierre Courtin: L'oeuvre gravé 1944-1972*, Paris: Yves Rivière, 1973

Rivière
Yves Rivière, *Serge Poliakoff: Les estampes*, Paris: Arts et Métiers Graphiques, 1974

Rivière
Yves Rivière, Georges Dubay, and Christian Labbaye, *Soulages: Eaux-fortes, lithographies 1952-1973*, Paris: Arts et Métiers Graphiques, 1974

Saphire and Cramer
Lawrence Saphire and Patrick Cramer, *André Masson: Catalogue raisonné des livres illustrés*, Geneva: Patrick Cramer, 1994

Schmücking
Rolf Schmücking, *Hans Hartung, Das Graphische Werk 1921-1965*, Braunschweig: Galerie Schmücking, 1965 (2nd edn, Basle, 1990)

Stedilijk
Victor Vasarely, Serigrafieën, Stedelijk Museum, Amsterdam, 1967

Vallotton-Goerg
Maxime Vallotton and Charles Goerg, *Félix Vallotton. Catalogue raisonné of the printed graphic work*, Geneva: Les Editions de Bonvent, 1972

Vallier
Dora Vallier, *Braque: L'Oeuvre gravé. Catalogue raisonné*, Lausanne: Flammarion, 1982

Völker
Brigitte Völker, *Henri Laurens: Werkverzeichnis der Druckgraphik*, Berlin: Edition Brusberg, 1985

Walterskirchen
Katalin von Walterskirchen, *Maurice de Vlaminck: Verzeichnis des graphischen Werkes*, Bern: Benteli Verlag, 1974

Webel
Sophie Webel, *L'Oeuvre gravé et les livres illustrés par Jean Dubuffet: catalogue raisoné*, 2 vols, Paris: Baudoin Lebon, 1991

Wittrock
Wolfgang Wittrock, *Yves Tanguy: Das Druckgraphische werk/ L'oeuvre gravé/ The graphic work*, Dusseldorf: Wolfgang Wittrock, 1976

GLOSSARY OF PRINTMAKING TERMS

For fuller explanations, see Antony Griffiths, *Prints and Printmaking: An introduction to the history and techniques*, (British Museum Press, London, 1996)

Aquatint
A variety of etching used to create tone. Resin particles are fused to the plate, which is then etched, the acid biting in the channels around each particle. These hold sufficient ink to print as an even tone.

Drypoint
A sharp needle, held like a pencil, is scratched directly into the metal plate. The metal residue, known as a burr, is pushed to either side of the incision; the burr, which easily wears under pressure from the press, retains the ink and produces a rich velvety line when the plate is printed.

Edition
Since the end of the 19th century, artists' prints have usually been printed in limited editions. These are published by dealers where the limitation of the edition artificially creates a market. Prior to printing an edition of 100, for instance, various trial proofs (*épreuves d'essai*) are pulled till one is reached which satisfies the artist's requirements. This proof, which the French call *bon-à-tirer* (good-to-pull), serves as the master print for judging the standard of each print in the subsequent edition. Each print from a limited edition is usually signed by the artist and inscribed with its number and edition size. As various technical processes are involved, an artist often collaborates with printers in workshops. While the artist works on the plate or stone, proofs are sometimes taken which record the different stages or *states*, in the making of the print.

Engraving
A V-shaped tool called a burin is pushed along the metal plate, producing a clean and crisp line. The plate is inked and printed in a similar way to an etching.

Etching
The artist draws freely with a metal point (known as an etching needle) through a hard waxy ground covering the metal plate. The exposed metal is then 'bitten' by acid. This can be done by immersing the plate in an acid bath or by painting parts of the plate with acid.

Intaglio
The basic principle of intaglio printmaking is that the line is incised into the metal plate. Ink is rubbed into the incised lines and the surface of the plate wiped clean. The plate is printed by placing a sheet of dampened paper over it and passing them through the press under heavy pressure. **Aquatint, drypoint, engraving, etching, mezzotint, soft-ground etching** and **sugar aquatint** are all intaglio techniques. The methods of printing are the same, but the result of each technique is different. A characteristic feature of the intaglio print is the plate mark impressed into the paper.

Linocut
The same process as for woodcut, except that linoleum is used instead of wood. In making his colour linocuts, Picasso developed the 'reductive' method, whereby a single block was cut and printed before further cutting and printing of the same block with the next colour.

Lithography
The technique of printing from stone or specially prepared zinc plates which relies on the antipathy of grease and water. The drawing is made with a greasy medium like crayon on the surface. The printing surface is dampened so that when greasy ink is applied it will adhere only to the drawn image and be repelled by water covering the rest of the stone or plate. The ink is transferred to a sheet of paper by passing paper and printing surface together through a scraper press. Instead of drawing directly on the stone, the artist can also use a special paper treated with a soluble surface on which the drawing is made with a greasy medium. The drawing can then be transferred to the stone or plate. This is known as **transfer lithography**.

Mezzotint

An intaglio technique where the metal plate is worked over with a multi-serrated tool, traditionally a rocker, so that the entire surface is roughened. In this state the plate would produce a uniform black if inked and printed. The image is formed by burnishing and scraping the roughened plate until varying degrees of smoothness are obtained. The smoother the plate, the less ink it will hold, so that a shiny area of plate will print as white, while the progressively rougher area will print as a range of deepening greys.

Monotype

As the name implies, only one, or at most two impressions, can be made by this technique in which ink is painted onto a flat surface such as metal or glass. Printing is achieved by rubbing the back of a sheet of paper placed onto the ink-covered surface.

Screenprinting

A variety of stencil printing. A mesh is attached tautly to a frame and the stencil, which may be made of cut paper, glue or a photographically developed film of gelatine, is fixed to the mesh, blocking it in some places and leaving it open elsewhere for the passage of ink. To make a print, a sheet of paper is placed underneath the frame and ink is carried across it by a rubber blade, known as a squeegee.

Soft ground

A type of etching which uses a soft etching ground. Paper may be placed over it. Where a line is drawn, the soft ground clings to the paper, leaving a facsimile of the drawing on the plate which is then etched in the usual way. Much used by artists at Atelier 17, this technique can also be used for pressing different surfaces onto the plate to create a variety of textures in the final print.

Stencil

A stencil print is made by applying colour through an area cut out of a paper or metal mask onto the paper below. In France this technique is known as *pochoir*.

Sugar aquatint

A type of aquatint which allows the artist to produce the design in positive brush strokes. After the plate has been prepared with resin, the image is brushed on to the plate using a special ink containing sugar. When almost dry the plate is overlaid with acid-resisting varnish and placed in a bath of warm water. Since the sugar varnish never completely dries, the water causes the varnish to lift, revealing the resin-covered design below which is ready to be bitten in the normal way.

Woodcut

A block, usually of plank wood revealing the grain, is cut with chisels and gouges so that the areas to be inked stand in relief. Ink is then rolled onto the surface of the block, which is then printed under vertical pressure in a press onto a sheet of paper. It can also be printed by hand-rubbing the back of the paper.

Wood-engraving

A type of woodcut where the block is cut across the grain of a closely grained wood, such as boxwood, which is too hard to be cut with a knife; a V-shaped burin is used instead to incise lines into the block. It is printed in the same way as a woodcut.

INDEX OF ARTISTS

References are to catalogue numbers